Biblical Studies from the Catholic Biblical Association of America

Previous Volumes in Biblical Studies from the CBA

1.
A Concise Theology of the New Testament
Frank J. Matera

2.
Letters to the Johannine Circle: 1–3 John
Francis J. Moloney, SDB

3.
The Landscape of the Gospels: A Deeper Meaning
Donald Senior, CP

4.
Scripture and Tradition in the Letters of Paul
Ronald D. Witherup, PSS

5.
Christ in the Book of Revelation
Ian Boxall

6.
Come and See: Discipleship in the Gospel of John
Sherri Brown

7.
The Theology and Spirituality of the Psalms of Ascents
Bradley C. Gregory

8.
Amos and Hosea: The Justice and Mercy of God
Katherine M. Hayes

9.
The Shape of Matthew's Story
Francis J. Moloney, SDB

10.
The Gospel of Mark: A Theological Reading
José Enrique Aguilar Chiu

11.
John the Baptizer: Reformer and Hinge of Scripture
Bonnie B. Thurston

A New and Living Way

Christ in the Letter to the Hebrews

Kevin B. McCruden

Biblical Studies
from the Catholic Biblical
Association

No. 12

Paulist Press
New York / Mahwah, NJ

Cover image by wichai bopatay/Shutterstock.com
Cover and book design by Lynn Else

Library of Congress Cataloging-in-Publication Data
Names: McCruden, Kevin B. author
Title: A new and living way: Christ in the Letter to the Hebrews / Kevin B. McCruden.
Description: New York: Paulist Press, [2025] | Series: Biblical studies from the Catholic Biblical Association of America; no. 12 | Includes bibliographical references.
Identifiers: LCCN 2024060726 (print) | LCCN 2024060727 (ebook) | ISBN 9780809154517 paperback | ISBN 9780809188741 ebook
Subjects: LCSH: Jesus Christ—Person and offices | Bible. Hebrews,—Criticism, interpretation, etc.
Classification: LCC BS2775.52 .M3355 2025 (print) | LCC BS2775.52 (ebook)
LC record available at https://lccn.loc.gov/2024060726
LC ebook record available at https://lccn.loc.gov/2024060727

ISBN 978-0-8091-5451-7 (paperback)
ISBN 978-0-8091-8874-1 (ebook)

Published by Paulist Press
997 Macarthur Boulevard
Mahwah, NJ 07430
www.paulistpress.com

Printed and bound in the
United States of America

For Tom

"He was a scholar, and a ripe and good one: Exceeding wise, fair-spoken, and persuading." *Henry VIII* 4.2.58–59

Contents

CONTENTS

About the Series

This series, Biblical Studies from the Catholic Biblical Association of America, seeks to bridge the gap between the technical exegetical work of the academic community and the educational and pastoral needs of the ecclesial community. Combining careful exegesis with a theological understanding of the text, the members of the Catholic Biblical Association of America have written these volumes in a style that is accessible to an educated, nonspecialized audience without compromising academic integrity.

These volumes deal with biblical texts and themes that are important and vital for the life and ministry of the Church. While some focus on specific biblical books or particular texts, others are concerned with important theological themes, still others with archaeological and geographical issues, and still others with questions of interpretation. Through this series, the members of the Catholic Biblical Association of America are eager to present the results of their research in a way that is relevant to an interested audience that goes beyond the confines of the academic community.

Preface

My first interest in the Letter to the Hebrews can be traced to my time spent as a doctoral student studying at Loyola University Chicago. It was there, inspired by the teaching of the department's New Testament faculty, that I first became intrigued by the many intellectual and theological challenges associated with this mysterious letter. Numerous aspects of Hebrews attracted my attention. Principal among these was the literary artistry of the text and the letter's curious reticence about its original audience and location. But more than anything else, I found myself drawn to the theological sophistication of the text. For here was a letter that gave expression to a Christology that, while as exalted as any found among the writings of the New Testament, was at the same time profoundly uncompromising in its representation of the humanity of Christ. Now years later, I am still persuaded that few texts from the New Testament capture such christological balance between the exalted and the human better than the Letter to the Hebrews does.

Now that this study is completed, I would like to express my gratitude both to Frank Matera and Enrique Aguilar for inviting me to contribute a thematic study of the priestly Christology of Hebrews for the new BSCBA. I would also like to thank Sheila McGinn, the new general editor of the series, for her encouragement to see this study through to the light of day. I am especially grateful to all three for the patience they extended to me to complete this project as I completed my second term as chair of the Department of

Religious Studies at Gonzaga University. I am also grateful to the administration at Gonzaga for granting me a sabbatical leave; it afforded me both the time and energy to begin this project and set it well on its way to its final completion. Finally, I would like to dedicate this volume to the Scripture faculty who were my teachers and mentors at Loyola University Chicago, especially Dr. Wendy Cotter, CSJ, Dr. David E. Aune, and Dr. Robert DiVito. As I write this preface, I am particularly mindful of the sudden and recent passing of Fr. Thomas Tobin, SJ. A great teacher, scholar, and an admirer of Hebrews, Tom encouraged me always to aim for clarity, accessibility, and, if possible, at least a small measure of elegance in whatever I might write. My sincere wish is that this study would have merited his approval.

Kevin B. McCruden
Gonzaga University
Spokane, WA

Introduction

The High Priestly Christology of the Letter to the Hebrews

One of my favorite scenes from the 1984 Academy Award winning film *Amadeus* portrays the court composer Antonio Salieri finding a manuscript left unattended by his younger contemporary, Wolfgang Amadeus Mozart. As Salieri scans the musical notation, the audience overhears the lovely melody playing in Salieri's mind, followed by Salieri's reaction to the melody: "This," says a visibly enraptured Salieri, "was a music I'd never heard." I think often of this scene whenever I recall my first experience with reading the Letter to the Hebrews. Although at the time I could not put my impression of the letter into words, I remember feeling that here was a portrayal of Jesus that I had never met before. It was only sometime later, following my introduction to the academic subject of Christology, that I discovered a more technical language to put my impression of this portrayal of Jesus into words. Nonetheless, it was the feeling that came first; the language needed to articulate the feeling took more time to catch up.

Christology is a term that biblical scholars employ to signify those conceptions of the identity and activity of Jesus that appear in the writings of the canonical New Testament.[1] Since the New Testament comprises diverse kinds of writings, it is important to recognize that no single Christology captures fully the variety of ways in which Jesus is perceived in the New Testament. For instance, while all four of the canonical Gospels portray Jesus as the divinely commissioned agent of God, each of the Gospels communicates this conviction in its own unique way.

Two examples from the New Testament might help illustrate this point. Together, the Gospel according to John and the Gospel according to Mark emphasize the importance of the death of Jesus for grasping the deeper significance of who he is in relation to God. At the same time, each of these narratives reflects on the significance of Jesus's death in different ways. In Mark's Gospel, Jesus's identity as God's Son stays hidden throughout much of the narrative. It is only when Jesus dies on the cross that his identity is definitively revealed, ironically by one of the soldiers who took part in his execution (Mark 15:39). This well-known element of secrecy that is so characteristic of Mark's Gospel contributes greatly to the dramatic tension that animates the plot of his story. But just as importantly, Mark's highlighting of secrecy also promotes a clear theological claim. By having the resolution of secrecy occur at the precise moment of Jesus's death on the cross, Mark draws the reader's attention to the explicit question concerning the deeper significance behind all that Jesus has said and done up until that point in the narrative. For Mark, the power of God's kingdom, as well

1. Christopher McMahon offers a concise and accessible definition of Christology: "The disciplined investigation into how Christians have identified and articulated the religious significance of Jesus is called Christology," in Christopher McMahon, *Reading the Gospels: Biblical Interpretation in the Catholic Tradition* (Winona, MN: Anselm Academic, 2012), 204.

as the mystery of who Jesus is as God's Son, is paradoxically most perceptible in an event of abject weakness.

In John's Gospel, by contrast, the identity of Jesus as the divine Word (John 1:1) is always on display, even in those situations where not every character perceives or even accepts the revelation of divine glory in him (John 1:9–14). Like Mark, the Fourth Gospel also views Jesus's death as a salvific event: "Now Jesus did many other signs in the presence of [his] disciples that are not written in this book. But these are written that you may [come to] believe that Jesus is the Messiah, the Son of God, and that through this belief you may have life in his name" (John 20:30–31).[2] But whereas Mark views Jesus's suffering and death as the prelude to his future glorification (Mark 14:62), John conceives of the suffering and death of Jesus as part of a grander process of glorification. This process begins with the event of Jesus's crucifixion and extends ultimately through the events of his resurrection and ascension (see John 12:23–24; 17:1–5). The Fourth Gospel thus views the death of Jesus as encompassing the first act in a far deeper divine drama that consists of his return to the Father: "Before the feast of Passover, Jesus knew that his hour had come to pass from this world to the Father. He loved his own in the world and he loved them to the end" (John 13:1).

Both evangelists, therefore, understand the suffering and death of Jesus to be inseparable from any truly authentic understanding of who he is. Nonetheless, each evangelist describes the significance of the suffering and death of Jesus in distinctive ways. A similar claim can be made about the unique christologies that are to be found in other New Testament writings. Indeed, to state this in slightly more metaphorical terms, if one were to think of Christology as a

2. All scriptural quotations are taken from the NABRE translation. I occasionally have modified the translation to use gender inclusive language.

kind of melody, diversity would be the dominant key that sounds across the New Testament.

Among the diverse expressions of Christology found throughout the New Testament, one of the most distinctive appears in the document known as the Letter to the Hebrews. From ancient times to the present, the unique witness of Hebrews to the ultimate meaning of the Christ event has engaged the imaginations of countless audiences. A key dimension of that witness pertains to Hebrews' depiction of Jesus as a high priest. Among the writings of the New Testament, only Hebrews ever calls Jesus by this title (2:17; 3:1; 4:14, 15; 5:1, 5, 10; 6:20; 7:26; 8:1; 9:11). Recognizing how very unusual it is to call Jesus a priest presents a useful place to begin our study on the priestly Christology of Hebrews.

In most instances in the New Testament where the terminology of priesthood appears, it refers to the hereditary office of the Jewish priesthood. The Jewish priests supervised the sacrificial cult, first in the portable sanctuary that accompanied the Israelites during the exodus journey (Exod 40:1–38), and then later in the great temple of Jerusalem during the time of Jesus's public ministry (circa 30–33 CE). In those few places in the New Testament where this is not the case, one sees priestly terminology functioning in a metaphorical, as opposed to a literal manner. That is, when the terminology of priesthood appears, it functions above all else to highlight the sacred, set-apart status of the community of Christ followers. This is a community that understands itself as rooted in and dedicated to the abiding presence of the resurrected Jesus living in their midst. A striking example of such a metaphorical usage appears in one of the letters of the Apostle Paul. Nearing the end of his correspondence addressed to the house churches in Rome, Paul speaks about what he understands to be his divinely bestowed vocation:

> But I have written to you rather boldly in some respects to remind you, because of the grace given me by God to be a minister of Christ Jesus to the Gentiles in performing the priestly service of the gospel of God, so that the offering up of the Gentiles may be acceptable, sanctified by the holy Spirit. (Rom 15:16)

In this passage, Paul envisions his calling to carry the salvific message about the death and resurrection of Jesus to the Gentile world as a holy vocation that is offered as a gift to God in the Holy Spirit (compare 1 Pet 2:5; Rev 1:6). A similar metaphorical usage of the language of priesthood also appears in the Letter to the Hebrews. Unlike what we see in Romans, however, Hebrews' use of the metaphor carries an explicitly communal connotation:

> We have an altar from which those who serve the tabernacle have no right to eat.... Through him [then] let us continually offer God a sacrifice of praise, that is the fruit of lips that confess his name. Do not neglect to do good and to share what you have; God is pleased by sacrifices of that kind. (13:10–16)

This passage belongs to a lengthier section in which Hebrews portrays Christ's sufferings—specifically the shedding of his blood—as consecrating the community (13:11–12). Additional priestly associations are further amplified by Hebrews' employment of the image of an altar (13:10) on the one hand, and by linking the concept of sacrifice (itself a priestly activity) to the communal performance of good works and praise of God, on the other (13:16).

Still, even in these instances of a metaphorical application, the vocabulary of priesthood never appears in Hebrews in connection with the person of Jesus. In fact, Hebrews is quite forthright in acknowledging that calling Jesus a priest signifies an innovation that requires explanation. Seeking to relate Jesus to the mysterious figure of Melchizedek who appears in both the book of Genesis and in Psalm 110 (see Gen 14:17–20; Ps 110:4), Hebrews notes the following:

> Now he of whom these things are said belonged to a different tribe, of which no member ever officiated at the altar. It is clear that our Lord arose from Judah, and in regard to that tribe, Moses said nothing about priests. (7:13–14)

Yet Hebrews insists not only that Jesus is a priest, but a high priest who has eternal status (7:15–16; 9:24), and who has offered a once-for-all sacrifice that has abolished sin (9:26–28; 10:11–12). One of the principal goals of this study will be to illustrate the essential features that make this priestly Christology of Hebrews one of the richest and most distinctive in all the New Testament.

THE CHALLENGE OF HEBREWS

The Letter to the Hebrews, for all of its christological distinctiveness, presents a number of interpretive challenges for readers of today. Particularly for those who might find themselves approaching the letter for the first time, its argumentation can at times seem unduly complex. For others, the challenge of Hebrews has less to do with its argumentative density than with the conceptualization of the cosmos that is assumed in the letter. Here is an ancient text that attributes a deeper level of truth to matters that are heavenly in nature, rather than earthly (9:23–24); invisible, rather than visible (11:1); eternal, rather than subject to time and change (7:22–24). The hope for the full arrival of the kingdom of God is, of course, also shared by many contemporary twenty-first century Christians. Still, the features of the cosmos that have been noted above probably held an even stronger resonance for a community whose members looked to the arrival of a heavenly reality perceived to be truer and more real than anything to be found in the visible world (see 11:13–16; 12:27–28; 13:14).

Stated another way, many have sensed in Hebrews a certain quality of remoteness, a remoteness that is only heightened by a portrayal of Christ that appears at least to privilege the exalted Christ at the expense of the human Jesus. Indeed, the impression that Hebrews is informed principally by a supremely high Christology is one that is shared by many readers.[3] Recognizing this, I intend to explore in this study whether the Christology of Hebrews does in fact minimize the humanity of Jesus, or whether Hebrews instead celebrates something more like a balance between the exalted and human aspects of Christ. I am convinced that the latter is more faithful to the spirit of the letter and, in the pages to follow, I hope to persuade the reader why I believe this to be the case.

I should clarify for the reader that these observations are not meant to dismiss or even to downplay the evident exalted dimension of the priestly Christology of Hebrews. Indeed, few other writings from the New Testament arguably convey as well as Hebrews does the transcendent depths of the mystery of the Christ event. To appreciate

3. Biblical scholars use the term *high Christology* to specify those portraits of Jesus in the writings of the New Testament that emphasize the divine identity of Christ. Few texts from the New Testament identify Jesus as God in any explicit sense. Hebrews would certainly be among such texts (1:8, 18), as would the Gospel according to John (1:1; 20:28). Texts that are more ambiguous in this regard include Rom 9:5, Tit 2:13, and 2 Pet 1:1.

the full texture of Hebrews' priestly presentation of the Christ event, however, it is crucial to explore the less familiar human dimension that is just as integral to the priestly Christology of the letter. Indeed, among the writings of the New Testament, the Letter to the Hebrews contains some of the most vividly drawn images of the humanity of Jesus. Only in Hebrews, for instance, do we find the affecting image of the tears that Jesus shed when he was facing the prospect of his own death (5:7). And perhaps no other New Testament writing apart from John's Gospel describes quite as graphically as Hebrews does the fully embodied nature of the incarnation. Much like what we see in the Prologue to John's Gospel, which describes the eternal Word becoming flesh and dwelling as a human person among fellow human beings (John 1:14), Hebrews also envisions the full humanity of the incarnate Son of God: "Now since the children share in blood and flesh, he likewise shared in them" (2:14; see also 2:18). In addition to the goal of sketching the broad contours of the priestly Christology of Hebrews, this study will highlight those places in the letter that specifically depict a human portrait of Christ, one that both complements and is held in tension with Hebrews' more exalted depiction of Christ.

APPROACHING HEBREWS FROM A CRITICAL THEOLOGICAL PERSPECTIVE

Whenever I first introduce my students to the critical study of Scripture, they often are surprised to discover that my use of the term *critical* amounts to a more formal way of saying that our time together will be spent exploring the

New Testament in an academic or scholarly way. Taking such a critical approach to a text like Hebrews requires that one approach the letter from the vantage point of a variety of scholarly perspectives. For example, there are available today many excellent studies that help illumine what one might call the conceptual background of Hebrews. Studies like these tend to be richly historical in content, alert to potential signals of both Jewish and Greco-Roman intellectual traditions that may have played a role in shaping the thematic subject matter of the letter. Other valuable studies—sharing a similar historical bent—look to situate Hebrews within its broader sociological or political context. Studies like these might analyze the way that Hebrews poses countercultural truth claims against the powerful sway of the Roman empire or offers a vision of alternative values that challenge the cultural status quo. Still other studies pursue a more literary approach to Hebrews by analyzing the rhetorical tools that were available to the author and lent both elegance and dynamism to the argumentative structure of the text. These latter studies helpfully illustrate that Hebrews is much more than just a text that is amenable to historical or sociological probing; it is also a document of persuasion, written both to inspire and challenge its audience. Such studies show that part of the beauty and power of Hebrews is the fact that this letter continues to challenge and inspire readers right down to today.

The primary approach that I will take in this study will be theological in nature. That is, I intend to explore religiously invested themes such as Hebrews' understanding of the nature of salvation, the personhood of Christ, and above all the interplay in the priestly Christology of Hebrews between the human and exalted dimensions of Christ's identity. At the same time, I recognize that giving attention to the historical, sociological, and literary aspects of Hebrews can only enrich and deepen the overall theological approach taken in this study.

For this reason, throughout this study I will periodically raise issues of historical, sociological, and literary significance that are relevant for the cultivation of a more complex understanding of Hebrews. This recognition acknowledges what today are regarded as best practices within Catholic biblical scholarship. When analyzing and interpreting any writing from the New Testament—including the Letter to the Hebrews—biblical scholars are encouraged to hold in creative tension two essential perspectives. These are (1) a commitment to the theological claim that the text of Scripture is indeed in some sense the word of God and (2) an awareness that the scriptural text is at the same time a thoroughly human writing, shaped by the limitations inherent to the time and culture in which it was written. As the word of God, Hebrews does indeed speak in a timely way to all readers of all times, as does all Scripture. This is why a writing like Hebrews can be viewed as having continuing relevance both for today and for the future. But it is just as important to recognize that Hebrews is not a timeless text, in the sense that it arose as a literary product written within, and written for, a specific first-century human community.

This study of the priestly Christology of Hebrews will unfold in four chapters with an accompanying conclusion. In chapter 1, I will supply a summary of the major background topics that contextualize the scholarly study of Hebrews today. These include observations regarding the audience and purpose of Hebrews; the authorship, date, and geographical location of the letter; and the literary form or genre of Hebrews. The remaining chapters will then be dedicated to providing an accessible account of the main features of the high priestly Christology of Hebrews. Following a definition of the concepts of sacrifice and atonement, the bulk of chapter 2 will focus on the theme of Christ's solidarity with humanity, a theme that animates the backdrop of the overall Christology of the letter. In chapter 3, I will focus on two additional themes that are also integral to Hebrews' portrait of Christ as a great high priest. These are (1) the human response of Jesus's faithfulness before God and its connection to the concept of the sinlessness of Jesus and (2) the compassion or empathy for humanity displayed by the exalted Christ. In the final chapter I will reflect on the connection that Hebrews makes between the exalted status of the risen Jesus and its relevance for the theme of human transformation. Finally, in the conclusion of the study, I will speak briefly on the topic of the timeliness of Hebrews, suggesting some ways that its priestly Christology might hold relevance for today.

Chapter One

Hebrews in Its Historical, Literary, and Pastoral Contexts

Biblical scholars who work with the texts of the New Testament do so with the aid of a variety of academic tools and methods that they have at their disposal. Those who focus on what many have described as the "world behind the text" strive to discover the varied historical dynamics that played a role in the generation of the texts of the New Testament. Such scholars address issues like the date, authorship, and geographical setting of specific New Testament writings, seeking to reconstruct the lived situation of the ancient audiences who were the first recipients of these texts.[1]

Since the writings contained in the New Testament were composed two thousand years ago, having emerged out of a social, cultural, and literary environment dissimilar from our own, historical analysis proves essential for engaging in responsible interpretation of these texts. The principal goal of such analysis aims at clarifying what the text was trying to say to its first audience. Roman Catholic biblical scholars often describe this goal as that of attend-

1. See the helpful and accessible discussion in Corrine L. Carvalho, *Primer on Biblical Methods* (Winona, MN: Anselm Academic, 2009), 1–29.

ing to the literal meaning of the text. In this instance, the word *literal* refers to what Christopher McMahon defines as "the meaning the ancient writers intended to express given their circumstances and their culture."[2] It is important to acknowledge, however, that finding answers to some of the historical questions we pose to ancient texts—including those contained in the New Testament—proves often to be a challenging and even at times impossible task. This is especially true when historical investigation involves guesswork about the lived situation of the ancient communities who first received these writings. The Letter to the Hebrews is no exception in this regard. Among the many important historical questions raised by this letter, those concerned with the makeup of the audience for Hebrews, as well as the purpose for which Hebrews might have been written, prove especially difficult to answer in any definitive manner.

THE WORLD BEHIND, THE WORLD OF, AND THE WORLD IN FRONT OF THE TEXT

The concepts of the world behind, the world of, and the world in front of the text denote different approaches that biblical scholars take when analyzing the writings of the New Testament. As already noted, questions involving the date, authorship, and cultural context of a given New Testament writing exemplify the approach known as the "world behind the text." By contrast, scholars who are attentive to the "world of the text" focus on the ways in which specific writings of the New Testament function as carefully crafted pieces of persuasive writing that have been designed to engage their audience. This approach is especially useful for exploring the

2. Christopher McMahon, *Reading the Gospels: Biblical Interpretation in the Catholic Tradition* (Winona, MN: Anselm Academic, 2012), 8.

canonical Gospels since the latter preserve the memories of Jesus's words and deeds within the format of a narrative or story. Last, we have the approach identified as the "world in front of the text." This approach builds on the other two approaches by exploring the ways in which readers of today might appropriate the writings of the New Testament within the context of their own time, place, and personal situation.

THE AUDIENCE AND PURPOSE OF HEBREWS

One might think that the title of the letter, "To the Hebrews," gives a reliable clue to the ethnic and religious identity of those who first received this letter. Unfortunately, since this title was attached to the letter no earlier than the late second century CE, it supplies little evidence about a community that likely received this letter in the latter part of the first century CE. Faced with such a situation, those who study Hebrews must analyze the actual contents of the letter, searching for any insight such analysis might yield about the original audience.

Distinguishing features of Hebrews, such as its extensive use of quotations from the Jewish Scriptures as well as its preoccupation with matters related to Jewish sacrificial ritual, convinced many scholars of an earlier generation that Hebrews addressed an audience originally comprised of Jewish Christ followers. This judgment, in turn, led scholars to envision the purpose of Hebrews as dissuading a community of recently converted Jews from abandoning their new commitment to Christ.[3] Two kinds of evidence

3. An eloquent proponent of this view is Barnabas Lindars. See Barnabas Lindars, *The Theology of the Letter to the Hebrews* (Cambridge: Cambridge University, 1991), 4–15.

were brought forward in support of this assessment: (1) Hebrews' criticism of what the author understood to be the inadequacy of Jewish sacrificial institutions (9:9–10, 13–14, 23–24; 10:4, 11) and (2) frequent cautionary warnings to the community highlighting the risk of falling away from their confessional commitment (2:1–3; 3:12; 4:1; 5:12; 10:23–27; 12:4–13, 25–26).

A NOTE ON TERMINOLOGY: THE JEWISH SCRIPTURES

For Christians today, both the Old and New Testament together constitute what functions as Sacred Scripture. It is worth acknowledging, however, that what Christians call the Old Testament is regarded by many contemporary Jews as simply the Jewish or Hebrew Scriptures. An alternate term that is sometimes used to name this body of ancient Jewish texts is the *TANAK*. The latter is an acronym that stands for the three main divisions of the Hebrew Bible: Torah, Prophets, and Writings. Today it is customary for biblical scholars to employ one of these alternate terms when referring to what Christians have traditionally called the Old Testament. In this study, I will follow this ecumenical practice and use the term *Jewish Scriptures* when referring to what Christians call the Old Testament.

Few scholars today are persuaded by this particular reconstruction of the audience and purpose of the letter. First, it is by no means certain that Hebrews was written with a Jewish audience in mind. The letter collection attributed to the Apostle Paul is instructive in this matter. This correspondence makes it explicitly clear that the communities founded by the Apostle to the Gentiles were composed chiefly of converted pagans who were ethnically Gentiles (see 1 Thess 1:9). In these letters, Paul takes for granted that at least some of his addressees would have been familiar with the scriptural passages that Paul uses to legitimate his advice (see 1 Cor 10:1–5; Rom 4:1–22). Something similar might apply to the audience for Hebrews; they also may have appreciated the complex development of scriptural themes and frequent use of scriptural citation that are both so characteristic of this letter.

There are, in fact, indications in the text that make the probability of a Gentile, pagan audience for the letter quite plausible. Midway through the letter, Hebrews urges its audience to advance beyond the foundation of what the author describes as "repentance from dead works" (6:1). While the meaning of this exhortation is not entirely clear, it might have served as an invitation to the community to recollect the moment of their initial conversion experience. If this suggestion is correct, the reference to "dead works and faith in God" is intended to inspire Hebrews' audience to recall the rejection of their polytheistic past. Paul employs a similar strategy in 1 Thessalonians when he rejoices that the Christ followers of Thessalonica are now included among those who have "turned to God from idols to serve the living and true God" (1 Thess 1:9). Here the idols that Paul envisions are the wooden or marble statues that were crafted to represent the numerous Greco-Roman deities worshipped throughout the ancient Mediterranean world.

None of these observations prove, of course, that the audience addressed by Hebrews was a community of recently converted pagans. In fact, with Hebrews we may have an instance of a text where the pursuit of a rigid separation between a Jewish and Gentile audience may prove in the end to be unhelpful for interpretation.[4] Addressing this question of the ethnic and religious identity of the original audience for Hebrews, Harold Attridge contends that perhaps the most one can say about the identity of the audience addressed by Hebrews is that they were a community experiencing "external pressure" or "persecution" (10:36—12:13), which resulted in "a waning commitment to the community's confession."[5]

We have already noted that the audience addressed by Hebrews was not necessarily a Jewish one. Neither is it necessary to draw the conclusion that Hebrews shows any awareness of a pressing danger of religious relapse threatening the community. Despite the strong indictment of Jewish sacrificial institutions visible in the letter (10:1–18), little certain evidence supports the claim that members of the community felt any doubt or misgivings regarding the sufficiency of Christ's sacrifice on their behalf (10:14–18). If there was any danger of apostasy, Hebrews seems to think of it either as a gradual falling away from commitment (2:1) or a slackening of endurance (10:36–39), and not as a return to former Jewish or even pagan beliefs. Following the lead of Attridge, it appears more helpful to interpret the warning passages that recur throughout Hebrews as summonses to the community to persevere in its faith commitment:

> Remember the days past when, after you had been enlightened, you endured a great contest of suffering. At times you were publicly exposed to

4. See Annette Yoshiko Reed, "Hellenistic Judaism beyond Judaism and Hellenism," in *Above, Below, Before, and After: Studies on Judaism and Christianity in Dialogue with Martha Himmelfarb*, ed. Ra'anan Boustan, David Frankfurter, and Annette Yoshiko Reed (Tübingen: Mohr Siebeck, 2023), 15-42.

5. Harold W. Attridge, *The Epistle to the Hebrews: A Commentary on the Epistle to the Hebrews* (Philadelphia: Fortress, 1989), 13.

> abuse and affliction; at other times you associated yourselves with those so treated. You even joined in the sufferings of those in prison and joyfully accepted the confiscation of your property, knowing that you had a better and lasting possession. (10:32–34)

Few passages in Hebrews illustrate more powerfully than this one does the evident distress experienced by members of the community addressed by this letter. While Hebrews envisions the traumatic loss of honorable status as an experience located in the audience's past, there are still other sections in the letter that reveal an author concerned to give pastoral support to a community that continues to experience flagging commitment in the present:

> We must consider how to rouse one another to love and good works. We should not stay away from our assembly, as is the custom of some, but encourage one another, and this all the more as you see the day drawing near. (10:24–25)

AUTHORSHIP, DATE, AND SETTING

Speculation about the possible authorship, date, and geographical setting of Hebrews continues to be a lively issue in scholarly study of the letter. Although sectors of the early Church wavered on the issue of the apostolic status of the letter, Hebrews eventually came to be included among the letters of Paul. This result owed largely to the advocacy of such prominent early Church writers as Jerome and Augustine in the western part of the empire. Each of these authors considered the overall message of Hebrews, if not the literary style, compatible with several of the theological emphases on display in Paul's other letters. By contrast, most contemporary scholars find the abundant thematic and stylistic differences that appear when one compares Hebrews to the letters of Paul as providing weighty evidence that Paul was not the actual author of the letter. The name Paul appears nowhere in the text of Hebrews, though one of Paul's major missionary companions, Timothy, is mentioned in the final chapter of the letter (see 13:23).

If not Paul, then who might the author have been? Responses to this question are often based on considerations either of the style of Hebrews, or on speculation about other missionary figures mentioned in other places in the New Testament as associates of Paul. For example, the elegant Greek of Hebrews leads some to consider Luke, whose Gospel also is marked by elevated Greek, as a potential candidate for authorship of Hebrews. The choice of Luke also has going for it the tradition that identified the author of Luke's Gospel as the traveling companion of Paul (see Col 4:14; Acts 16:11). Since the time of the Middle Ages, another popular candidate has been the figure of Apollos, who worked alongside Paul, as well as independently of him (see 1 Cor 3:4–22; 16:12). Apollos also makes an appearance in the Book of Acts, part two of the larger two-volume work that includes the Gospel of Luke. The notice about Apollos in Acts is especially interesting since it emphasizes Apollos' skill in the art of persuasive public speaking: "A Jew named Apollos, a native of Alexandria, an eloquent speaker, arrived in Ephesus. He was an authority on the scriptures. He had been instructed in the Way of the Lord and, with ardent spirit, spoke and taught accurately about Jesus, although he knew only the baptism of John" (Acts 18:24–25). Since Hebrews shows the strongest evidence of an author familiar with the principles of Greco-Roman oratorical theory, the choice of Apollos is intriguing to say the least. However, these choices, as well as other potential candidates for authorship of Hebrews, amount to little more than educated guesses.[6] While the author of Hebrews was likely known to the first recipients of the letter (see 13:19, 22), from this historical distance it is impossible to know with any certainty who this person actually was. For this reason, it is best to consider Hebrews as one among several anonymous texts that came to be included in the New Testament.

HEBREWS' UNCERTAIN AUTHORSHIP

Origen's oft-noted reflections on the question of the authorship of Hebrews are preserved in the sixth book of the *Church History* of Eusebius of Caesarea, which was written in the early fourth century.

"But again, on the other hand, that the thoughts of the epistle are admirable, and not inferior to the acknowledged writings of the apostle, to this also everyone will consent as true who has given attention to reading the apostle....But as for myself, if I were to state my own opinion, I should say that the thoughts are the apostle's, but that the style and composition belonged to one who called to mind the apostle's teachings and, as it were, made short notes of what his master said. If any church, therefore, holds this epistle as Paul's, let it be commended for this also. For not without reason have the men of old handed it down as Paul's. But who wrote the epistle, in truth God knows. Yet the account which has reached us [is twofold], some saying that Clement, who was bishop of the Romans, wrote the

6. Alan Mitchell has supplied a helpful summary of some of the ancient, medieval, and modern guesses on the authorship of Hebrews. See Alan C. Mitchell, *Hebrews*, Sacra Pagina Series 13 (Collegeville, MN: Liturgical Press, 2007), 2–6.

epistle, others, that it was Luke, he who wrote the Gospel and the Acts" (*Church History* 6.25.14).

As is the case with all the New Testament writings, Hebrews does not supply us with explicit data regarding its date of composition. The earliest existing copies of Hebrews in its original Greek language date from around the year 200 CE, though the letter certainly was written well before then. There are potential clues in the letter, however, that make it possible to establish what amounts to an approximate timeframe for the composition of Hebrews. Craig Koester, for instance, points to passages (2:3; 10:32–34; 13:23) that seem to envision an audience made up primarily of second-generation Christ followers. If Koester's observation is correct, that would mean that Hebrews was written subsequent to the first wave of evangelism that took place in the 40s and 50s CE, but before the close of the first century CE.[7] Attempts at dating Hebrews more precisely than this face the uncertainty over whether Hebrews appeared either before, or sometime after, the destruction of the temple in Jerusalem in the year 70 CE. Alan Mitchell argues persuasively for dating Hebrews sometime after the temple's destruction. A frequently noted feature of Hebrews is that it neither mentions the Jerusalem temple nor links its statements concerning sacrifice and priesthood to contemporary practices in the temple. Hebrews focuses instead on the portable tent that was said to have accompanied the Israelites during their period of wandering in the wilderness as recounted in the Books of Exodus and Leviticus. According to Mitchell, the fact that Hebrews depicts the nonpriest Jesus (7:14) explicitly as a high priest without ever referring to the physical temple is best accounted for by the

7. Craig R. Koester, *Hebrews: A New Translation with Introduction and Commentary*, Anchor Bible 36 (New York: Doubleday, 2001), 50.

absence of the temple and its priestly personnel at the time the letter was written.[8] Additional evidence in support of a post–70 CE date for Hebrews is the letter's strong replacement/fulfillment theme regarding Jewish religious institutions, especially those associated with the ritual sacrifice (10:1–15). A similar replacement/fulfillment theme is characteristic of the Fourth Gospel, which is considered by most scholars to be the latest of the four New Testament Gospels to have been completed, near the end of the first century. A late first-century date for the composition of Hebrews therefore seems plausible.

Hebrews reveals neither its intended destination nor the location from which it may have been sent. If chapter 13 was originally part of the letter and not, as some have argued, added to the finished text of Hebrews sometime later, a potential clue regarding destination might be found near the conclusion of the letter: "Greetings to all your leaders and to all the holy ones. Those from Italy send you greetings" (13:24). While much debated among scholars, this verse appears to envisage a scenario in which Christ followers are sending greetings to fellow Christ followers who are living somewhere in Italy, even perhaps in Rome. Given that there was already a robust Christian presence in the capital of the empire by the time Paul wrote to the Roman Christ followers in the mid-fifties of the first century, Rome is a good, though ultimately unverified candidate for the possible destination for Hebrews.

LITERARY GENRE: WHAT KIND OF A WRITING IS HEBREWS?

Settling on a decision apparently as uncomplicated as identifying the literary genre to which Hebrews belongs

---

8. Mitchell, *Hebrews*, 9–11.

proves to be a surprisingly challenging task. Hebrews' location in the canon, coming at the end of the letter collection of Paul, suggests that from an early date Hebrews was associated with the literary genre of the ancient letter. Ancient letters, such as those written by Paul, tended to adhere to a fixed format that included such features as the listing of the sender and recipient of the letter, as well as the inclusion of a short thanksgiving section (see Phil 1:1–10). Hebrews famously concludes, in chapter 13, with a series of general exhortations along with a final greeting (13:24). Both these were customary features of ancient correspondence. Hebrews begins, however, without including any of the ancient conventions considered customary for a proper way to begin a letter: neither the sender, nor the addressee, nor a thanksgiving appears. Mindful of both the absence of these formal elements as well as the author's own description of the letter as a "word of exhortation" (13:22), some have suggested that Hebrews might best be thought of less as a letter and more as an example of an ancient sermon with only hints of a letter format—a mixed genre, as it were.

Conceiving of Hebrews as an example of an ancient sermon complements important features of the letter. For example, some of the imagery and thematic content that appears in Hebrews also appears in other examples that have been preserved of ancient speeches. These include the use of maritime imagery (2:1; 6:19), agricultural metaphors (6:7–8), and educational motifs (5:12–14; 12:5–7). Hebrews also shows a consistent preference for the activity of speech. The opening verses of the letter, for instance, portray God as speaking provisionally in the past but now definitively in the present (1:1–2). Hebrews likewise depicts God the Father and the Son engaging in dialogue with each other (1:5–13; 2:12–13; 5:5; 7:21; 10:5–9). And Hebrews often introduces scriptural citations as dramatic speech events (2:6, 11–13; 3:7; 4:3, 7;

5:6; 7:17, 21; 8:7; 10:5, 15–17). The anonymous author of Hebrews even at times engages directly with the audience as if present among them (5:11; 9:5; 13:22). All these features give added persuasiveness to the proposal that Hebrews is best conceived of as a sermon, or at the very least, a letter that is at its heart deeply homiletic.

PRIESTLY CHRISTOLOGY IN A PASTORAL KEY

An appreciation for the homiletic quality of Hebrews touches once again on the observation made earlier concerning the pastoral dimension of Hebrews' Christology. While many readers come away from their first encounter with Hebrews with a renewed appreciation for the sophistication of its theological vision, fewer perhaps find themselves struck by the impression that behind this letter is a gifted homilist, one who challenges his or her readers to think about the Christ event in a new way. Hebrews ultimately achieved canonical status, at least in part, because early Christians felt empowered by its unique and emotionally powerful witness to the deeper meaning of the Christ event. No small part of that empowerment was connected to how this sermon shaped and was in turn shaped by the lived experience of a community of early Christ followers. In anticipation of the chapters to follow, I will bring this first chapter to its conclusion by briefly exploring how this concern for lived experience accounts for the pastoral dimension of the priestly Christology of Hebrews.

It is important to recognize that Hebrews, along with so many examples of the writings found in the New Testament, was written for a community that occupied a marginalized place within the surrounding Greco-Roman culture.

While nothing like a precise number is available, there may have been approximately only a few thousand Christ followers living at the time Hebrews was written in the latter half of the first century. Given that the number of Christians today is estimated at over two billion, it is difficult to imagine a period in history with such a comparatively small number of Christ followers.

Whatever the actual demographic of Christ followers may have been at the time Hebrews was written, those belonging to the community addressed by this letter would have found themselves socially, religiously, and culturally in the minority. And just like many minority populations today, these early communities would have met with almost daily opposition and prejudice from both neighbors and acquaintances in the surrounding culture. Not all forms of opposition and prejudice would have entailed physical persecution. Social marginalization in the shape of societal scorn was perhaps the most common form of persecution experienced by the earliest Christ followers. The reason they received such treatment was quite simple. From the perspective of both ordinary and elite pagan citizens, to turn away from the worship of the traditional deities was to put the welfare of the city into jeopardy. And since religious piety was tied so closely to family values and civic virtue, converts from paganism risked being labeled as dishonorable persons. Deemed as such, they inevitably endured the stress of societal shaming.[9] In a way comparable to Paul, who likewise often found himself obliged to think of ways to offer encouragement and guidance to persecuted Christ followers (see, e.g., 1 Thess 2:1–14), Hebrews also strives to engage, comfort, and above all empower the collective imagination of its audience. Hebrews pursues this task

9. See David A. De Silva, *The Letter to the Hebrews in Social-Scientific Perspective*, Cascade Companions (Eugene, OR: Cascade, 2012), 45–58.

christologically, portraying Christ in ways that are crafted to surprise, challenge, and give hope to a community struggling to persevere in its commitment to Christ. In this way, Hebrews seeks to assure its audience about the empowering source of its salvation that is Christ, despite the potential cost that this commitment poses for their day-to-day lives (5:9).

PASTORAL CARE AS A STRUCTURING PRINCIPLE IN HEBREWS

Due to the complexity of the overall argument of Hebrews, attempts to supply a comprehensive outline that accounts for all the thematic content in the letter is a daunting task. Nonetheless, many scholars have noted an alternating pattern between more thematic material devoted largely to christological explication and material of a more hortatory character. The latter highlights the important place that pastoral care for the community occupied in the letter.

2:1–4	Exhortation to hold firmly to the message of salvation
3:7—4:11	Warnings against falling into unfaithfulness
5:11—6:12	Plea for renewed attention and striving for a mature faith
10:19–39	Exhortation to common life and endurance under stress
12:1–29	Exhortation to faith
13:1–19	Final exhortations relating to common life

Perhaps another way to put this is to suggest that the anonymous author of Hebrews seeks to persuade its audience not simply on a cognitive level, but on an emotional, affective level as well. Imagine the emotional and psychological effect that hearing the title of high priest applied to Jesus might have had on the members of this community. While they may have been surprised to hear it, they would have been familiar with the institution of the priesthood in its Jewish or Greco-Roman form. In addition to its religious importance, the institution of the priesthood in the ancient world brought significant prestige and honor to the celebrant. The honorable status attaching to the office of priesthood helps explain why, for example, in the iconography of the Roman imperial period, the depiction of sacrificial ritual is linked almost exclusively to the person of the Roman emperor, a figure whom most in the ancient world would have viewed as occupying the uppermost rung of the social honor ladder.[10] As we will discuss in more detail in the next chapter, through its rich use of visual imagery, Hebrews successfully depicts for its audience something like a literary iconography of Jesus's high priesthood that rivals any physical iconography that an ancient audience may have witnessed in their daily lives.[11] We see something similar when we turn our attention to the even more relevant Jewish context. The lofty reputation that attended the Jewish high priestly office is perhaps nowhere more eloquently expressed than in this passage taken from the second century BCE text entitled the Wisdom of Ben Sira:

> Greatest of his family, the glory of his people, was Simeon the priest....How splendid he was as he

10. See Richard Gordon, "The Veil of Power: Emperors, Sacrificers, and Benefactors," in *Pagan Priests: Religion and Power in the Ancient World*, ed. Mary Beard and John North (Ithaca, NY: Cornell University, 1990), 201–31.

11. This point is stated exceptionally well by Harry O. Maier. See Harry O. Maier, "For Here We Have No Lasting City (Heb 13:14a): Flavian Iconography, Roman Imperial Sacrificial Imagery, and the Epistle to the Hebrews," in *Hebrews in Contexts*, ed. Gabriella Gelardini and Harold W. Attridge, Ancient Judaism and early Christianity 91 (Leiden: Brill, 2016), 133–54.

> looked out from the tent, as he came from behind the veil! Like a star shining among the clouds, like the full moon at the festal season; like sun shining upon the temple of the King; like a rainbow appearing in the cloudy sky....Wearing his glorious robes, and vested in sublime magnificence, as he ascended the glorious altar and lent majesty to the court of the sanctuary. (Sir 50:1–11)

We see in this passage how the clothing and even the physical movement of the high priest are invested with an almost cosmic significance. Another example that illustrates the honorable aura understood to surround the office of the Jewish high priesthood, and one that is closer to the time that Hebrews was written, comes from the famous Jewish philosopher Philo of Alexandria. Philo has this to say about the ideal high priest:

> For when, the scriptures say, "the high priest goes into the Holy of Holies he will not be a man." What then will he be if he is not a man? Will he be God? I would not venture to say that...nor again is he man, but he touches both these extremities as if he touched both the feet and head. (*Dreams* 2.189–93)

According to Philo, the high priest, while thought of as a human being, nonetheless has the trappings of the divine.

It seems to me that the esteem and honor that went with the office of the priesthood in the ancient world helps to potentially illumine those passages in Hebrews that recall the historical memory of the humiliation and shame that Jesus endured during his passion. In one of the final sections of exhortation delivered in the letter, Hebrews urges its audience to join in keeping "our eyes fixed on Jesus, the leader and perfector of faith. For the sake of the joy that lay before him he endured the cross, despising its shame, and has taken his seat at the right hand of God" (12:2). This same Jesus, Hebrews declares, "also suffered outside the gate, to consecrate the people by his own blood. Let us then go to him outside the camp, bearing the reproach he bore" (13:12–13).

When one considers the identification of Jesus as a high priest against the background of passages like these, it becomes all the clearer that one of the functions of Hebrews' priestly Christology was to address the terrible scandal of the cross. Left unspoken behind the highly celebratory claims made about Jesus in Hebrews are echoes of contrary claims leveled against Christ followers by those who did not share the faith convictions of the former. These unsympathetic claims undoubtedly highlighted the dishonorable and shameful status of a person who suffered the ultimate degradation of a Roman execution by crucifixion. Indeed, one does not need to listen all too strenuously to hear behind the affirmation that Jesus was "holy," "innocent," "undefiled," and "separated from sinners" (7:26) a contrary claim to the effect that Jesus was a defiled and unholy figure; he certainly was not the kind of a person one would think would be vindicated by being raised to the divine realm as a consequence of having suffered such a degrading death. One of the motivations behind Hebrews' affirmation that Jesus was sinless (4:15) may very well have been the need to address precisely the claim that Jesus was rejected by God.

Directed to an audience of beleaguered Christ followers, Hebrews' priestly portrayal of Jesus would have served an important emotional, psychological, and eminently pastoral purpose. While this image of Christ as high priest would not have erased the tragedy and trauma of the cross, it could perhaps help to reconfigure for early Christ followers the dishonorable implications of the cross. Through such a project of reconfiguration of the death of Jesus, Hebrews would have succeeded in providing for its audience the emotional sustenance necessary for continuing to persevere in their countercultural faith, even if such commitment brought with it a reputational cost to their lives:

> At times you were publicly exposed to abuse and affliction; at other times you associated yourselves with those so treated. You even joined in the sufferings of those in prison and joyfully accepted the confiscation of your property, knowing that you had a better and lasting possession. (10:33–34)

Hebrews endeavors to inspire its audience to see in the Jesus who was crucified not a humiliated victim, but instead an eternal high priest who surpasses in honor and dignity all manner of other priests. Although we cannot know for certain if the author of Hebrews was familiar with any of the Apostle Paul's writings, it is not difficult to imagine that the author would have appreciated the triumphant claim that Paul makes in Romans 1:16: "For I am not ashamed of the gospel. It is the power of God for the salvation of everyone who believes." Like Paul, the author of Hebrews also sought to provide comfort to a community of early Christ followers who, owing to their marginalized status, were forced to contend daily with feelings of shame and disempowerment. An echo of both feelings can be heard in this passage found near the conclusion of the letter. Referring to the example Jesus, the author calls on the community to "consider how he endured such opposition from sinners, in order that you may not grow weary and lose heart" (12:3).

Through the use of extensive passages of sustained moral exhortation (2:1–4; 3:1–19; 4:1–14; 6:1–12; 10:19–39; 12:1–17), direct personal appeal (3:12–19; 5:11–14; 6:9–12; 10:32–39; 12:7–13), and reminders of all that they have been given in Christ (4:15; 6:19–20; 8:1–2; 10:10; 2:17–18; 3:1; 12:22–24), Hebrews invites its audience to invest themselves personally in the story told in this sermon regarding the divine intention of bringing "many children to glory" (2:10). For all these reasons, we might do better to describe the Christology of Hebrews as celebratory and pastoral, as opposed to abstract and systematic. Like a good homilist, the author of Hebrews is aware of the struggles the community is experiencing. And because of this awareness, the author attempts to meet the community in the painful place they inhabit with a message of hope and a summons to persevere (12:3–4, 35–39).

SUMMING UP THE HISTORICAL, LITERARY, AND PASTORAL CONTEXTS OF HEBREWS

Although Hebrews was associated as early as the third century CE with the Apostle Paul, both stylistic as well as thematic differences between Hebrews and Paul's letters rule out Paul as the likely author of the letter. Ultimately, it is best to view Hebrews as an anonymous writing.

Hebrews was probably written in the latter part of the first century, probably sometime after the destruction of the temple in Jerusalem, which took place in the year 70 CE.

Both the place of origin, as well as the destination for Hebrews, are unknown. Geographical signals within the text may point to a community living in Italy, perhaps in Rome.

A NEW AND LIVING WAY

The designation of Hebrews as a letter is somewhat misleading, since the text reads much more like a sermon designed to be read aloud.

While the priestly Christology of Hebrews is conceptually complex, a clear pastoral motivation nonetheless shapes the portrayal of Jesus as a great high priest.

Chapter Two

A Mediator Who Draws Near

PRELIMINARY OBSERVATIONS ON THE CONCEPTS OF SACRIFICE AND ATONEMENT

The importance that Hebrews assigns to the atoning significance of Christ's death appears early in the letter and from then on occupies a central place in the priestly Christology of the letter: "When he had accomplished purification [*katharismon*] from sins, he took his seat at the right hand of the Majesty on high" (1:3c). The terminology of purification here, as well as in other places in Hebrews (9:14, 20, 23; 10:2), attests to the strong influence that the Jewish concept of sacrificial atonement exercised on the author. In part, this influence is explained by the thoroughly Jewish matrix in which the reform movement that would later become Christianity originally appeared. In their effort to come to terms with the significance of the death of Jesus, the first Christ followers drew heavily from the religious symbols that were already available to them in the Jewish Scriptures. Among these symbols was the concept of atonement, which essentially implies the state of being reconciled with God. The animating belief behind the idea of reconciliation was the faith conviction that the death and resurrection of Jesus had made it possible for the faithful to live in a renewed way. As a result of being reconciled with God, the believer was now empowered to live a transformed life at peace with God and one's neighbor. Hebrews captures this sense of empowerment and transformation in the following passage:

> Therefore, brothers [and sisters], since through the blood of Jesus we have confidence of entrance into the sanctuary by the new and living way he opened for us through the veil, that is, his flesh, and since we have a great priest over the house of God, let us approach with a sincere heart and in absolute trust, with our hearts sprinkled clean from an evil conscience and our bodies washed in pure water. Let us hold unwaveringly to our confession that gives us hope, for he who made the promise is trustworthy. We must consider how to rouse one another to love and good works. We should not stay away from our assembly, as is the custom of some, but encourage one another, and this all the more as you see the day drawing near. (10:19–25)

It is important to note, however, that the general concept of sacrifice was not restricted to the Jewish Scriptures. Even in the broader setting of the Greco-Roman world, the practice of sacrifice formed an indelible feature of authentic piety. Despite differences in religious practice and belief, most Jews and pagans living in the time of the first century would have naturally associated the religious sphere with the tangible realities of altars, temples, and the ritual slaughter of animals.

The custom of offering sacrifice in antiquity functioned in much the same way that gift giving functions today within the context of interpersonal relationships. For example, when I give a gift to a friend or loved one, I am testifying to a bond that ties both of us together. And if the bond is an especially intimate or important one, I inevitably will give thought to the quality of the gift I give, ensuring that it is special or valuable in some way. Working from this analogy, one might similarly understand the institution of sacrifice in the ancient world as a form of gift giving—only, in this instance, the gift being offered to the deity is a gift bestowed by a human being.

The situations in life that served as occasions for the conferring of sacrificial gifts were varied. One might, for example, arrange for a sacrifice to be given on one's behalf to express thanksgiving for a blessing received, to confirm or solemnize a vow, or simply to show one's personal devotion (see Lev 7:11–18). In each of these examples, the sacrifice being offered stood for an embodied, concrete gift freely given by the worshipper to the deity. In the Greco-Roman world such sacrifices took place in public as well as private settings, and were conducted by ordinary persons, as well as by specially designated priests. Whereas animals were the frequent choice for sacrifice in both the Greco-Roman and Second Temple Jewish period, other items, including varieties of crops, also served as materials for offerings. Most forms of sacrifice were heavily ritualized. That is, they were governed by prescribed sets of rules relating to such activities as the handling of blood, purificatory washings, the burning of at least a part of the sacrificial offering, and the consumption of the sacrifice.

Many of the features that characterized Greco-Roman sacrifices were also features of Jewish sacrifices, although there were key differences as well. Whereas pagans offered sacrifices to a host of divine beings (including the Roman emperor), Jews of the Second Temple period regarded the sacrifices that they performed as being offered to the one true God, the God of Israel. In the Greco-Roman world, sacrifices took place in both public and private settings. During the lifetime of Jesus, by contrast, the expectation was that Jewish sacrifices were to take place solely in the temple in Jerusalem. And while in the Greco-Roman world a variety of persons could offer sacrifices, in the Jewish context only certain Jews, specifically males of Levitical descent (Exod 29:1–8), could serve as priests and oversee sacrificial ritual.

Since the author of Hebrews works with a concept of sacrifice that is explicitly built on a scriptural foundation, it makes sense to focus our discussion on the way sacrifice is described in these Jewish sources. Turning to the Jewish Scriptures, we see that distinct categories of sacrifices are mentioned along with specific kinds of sacrifice linked to distinctive goals (see Lev 1:1—7:38). One type that appears often is the so-called purification or sin offering. This sacrifice required the ritualized slaughter and shedding of an animal's blood in a cultic setting, usually a sanctuary of some kind, and was administered by a hereditary caste of Jewish priests. The purification offering was thought to address transgressions that occurred within the context of the covenant relationship set up by the God of Israel with the Jewish people. An analogy from human experience might help clarify this point. All of us are aware that the trials and challenges that often are a part of human interpersonal relationships can, if left unaddressed, pose obstacles to continued growth in relationship. Something like this seems to inform the logic behind the purification offering. Foundational to the act of sacrificial offering is the conviction that the God of Israel graciously makes provision in the law to address the inevitable lapses that are bound to arise in the day-to-day observance of one's covenantal obligations. In the lives of religiously observant Jews of the first century, the performance of sacrifice, together with repentance, played an embodied, concrete role in terms of the mending of breaches in the covenant relationship due to human transgression or sin.[1]

SECOND TEMPLE JUDAISM

The period in Jewish history spanning from 538 BCE to approximately 70 CE is sometimes named the Second Temple period. The first temple built in Jerusalem by King David's son, Solomon, was destroyed by the Babylonians in 586 BCE. Following this destruction, a significant proportion of the population of Judea was sent into exile in Babylon. A second temple would later be built in the year 515 BCE. This temple was destroyed in the year 70 CE by the Roman legions under the command of the Roman general Titus, shortly before the conclusion of the first Jewish-Roman war in 73 CE.

The Jewish Scriptures articulate the idea of the covenant restoration through the concept of expiatory atonement. This concept refers to the belief that the shed blood of a sacrificial animal, when handled in a ritually prescribed manner, can cleanse away sin. The concept is illustrated in the following passage from Hebrews: "According to the law almost everything is purified by blood, and without the shedding of blood there is no forgiveness" (9:22). Although the precise manner by which the expiatory power of atonement

1. See E. P. Sanders, *Paul and Palestinian Judaism: A Comparison of Patterns of Religion* (Minneapolis: Fortress Press, 1977), 180.

was thought to work is never made explicit in the Jewish Scriptures, it is clear that atonement was understood to result in the forgiveness of sin or transgression.[2] In turn, forgiveness of sin resulted in the restoration of covenant status with God:

> When someone is guilty in regard to any of these matters, that person shall confess the wrong committed, and make reparation to the LORD for the wrong committed: a female animal from the flock, a ewe lamb or a she-goat, as a purification offering. Thus, the priest shall make atonement on the individual's behalf for the wrong. (Lev 5:5–6; see also Lev 4:26, 31, 35)

Perhaps the most dramatic of all atoning sacrifices found in the Jewish Scriptures is the sacrifice linked to the Jewish festival known as the Day of Atonement or *Yom Kippur*. This was the day mandated by the Jewish law for the high priest to offer sacrifice for the cleansing of his own sin, as well as for the sins of the people. As described in the Book of Leviticus, the annual festival included a ceremony where the high priest entered alone into the innermost part of the portable tent or sanctuary that had been constructed following the events of the exodus from Egypt. Once inside the tent, the high priest sprinkled a portion of the blood of two sacrificed animals on the cover of the ark of the covenant. This was the place where it was believed the invisible presence of the God of Israel dwelled (Exod 35—40; Lev 16:1–2). The ritual handling and application of blood by the high priest

2. It seems that the concept of atonement bears some kind of connection with the assumption that blood is at the center of life: "Since the life of the flesh is in the blood, and I have given it to you to make atonement on the altar for yourselves, because it is the blood as life that makes atonement" (Lev 17:11–12).

was thought to effect two things: first, the purification of the sanctuary, and second, the expiation or cleansing of the collective sins of the people:

> Thus shall Aaron offer his bull for the purification offering, to make atonement for himself and for his family....Taking some of the bull's blood, he shall sprinkle it with his finger on the front of the ark's cover and likewise sprinkle some of the blood with his finger seven times in front of the cover. Then he shall slaughter the goat of the people's purification offering, and bringing its blood inside the veil, he shall do with it as he did with the bull's blood, sprinkling it on the ark's cover and in front of it. Thus he shall purge the inner sanctuary of all the Israelites' impurities and trespasses, including all their sins. He shall do the same for the tent of meeting, which is set up among them in the midst of their uncleanness. No one else may be in the tent of meeting from the time he enters the inner sanctuary to make atonement until he departs. When he has made atonement for himself and his household, as well as for the whole Israelite assembly, he shall come out to the altar before the LORD and purge it also. Taking some of the bull's and the goat's blood, he shall put it on the horns around the altar, and with his finger sprinkle some of the blood on it seven times. Thus he shall purify it and sanctify it from the impurities of the Israelites. (Lev 16:11–19)

It is clear that the ritual activity of the Jewish high priest on the Day of Atonement made a powerful impression on the author of Hebrews. One of the letter's clearest allusions to the ritual appears in the following passage:

> With these arrangements for worship, the priests, in performing their service, go into the outer tabernacle repeatedly, but the high priest alone goes into the inner one once a year, not without blood that he offers for himself and for the sins of the people....But when Christ came as high priest of the good things that have come to be, passing through the greater and more perfect tabernacle not made by hands, that is, not belonging to this creation, he entered once for all into the sanctuary, not with the blood of goats and calves but with his own blood, thus obtaining eternal redemption. (9:6–7, 11–12)

Two details stand out in this passage that merit further analysis. The first concerns the prominence given to the personal dimension of the sacrifice of Jesus: "he entered once for all into the sanctuary, not with the blood of goats and calves but with his own blood, thus obtaining eternal redemption" (9:12). In emphasizing the personal commitment of Jesus, Hebrews expresses the conviction that Jesus's sacrifice encompassed not just his death, but his entire life of faithfulness that culminated in his suffering, death, and exaltation.[3] The second detail concerns the author's priestly portrayal of Jesus. Not only does Hebrews envision Christ as an officiating high priest, but a high priest of a unique sort. Christ, the high priest, enters not into an earthly sanctuary,

3. A similar point is emphasized by Albert Vanhoye, who likewise points to the deeply embodied dimension of Jesus's passion. See Albert Vanhoye, SJ, *The Letter to the Hebrews: A New Commentary*, trans. Leo Arnold, SJ (Mahwah, NJ: Paulist Press, 2015), 143.

but a heavenly one, appearing face-to-face before the very presence of God (9:24). The priestly Christology of Hebrews illustrates, therefore, two striking theological claims unique to this letter. First, Jesus's sacrifice takes place in a heavenly, not an earthly sanctuary. Second, the one who is sacrificed is at the same time the one who carries out the sacrifice: "For if the blood of goats and bulls and the sprinkling of a heifer's ashes can sanctify those who are defiled so that their flesh is cleansed, how much more will the blood of Christ, who through the eternal spirit offered himself unblemished to God, cleanse our consciences from dead works to worship the living God" (9:13–14). For the author of Hebrews, then, Jesus is a special kind of high priest, one who offers his own self to God within the transcendent realm of heaven itself (9:24–25). While it is of course possible to point to other New Testament writings that employ sacrificial imagery to interpret the deeper significance of the suffering and death of Jesus (see, e.g., John 1:29; Rom 3:21–26; 1 Pet: 1:18–19), no other text apart from Hebrews describes the significance of the Christ event in such highly personal terms.

SACRIFICIAL LANGUAGE IN THE NEW TESTAMENT

A variety of texts in the New Testament attest to a sacrificial appraisal of the Christ event. Some of these texts are quite early, dating to the time of the ministry of Paul (see Rom 3:25; 1 Cor 5:7, 28), while others are nearer in time to when Hebrews was most likely written (see Acts 15:9; John 1:29; 1 Pet 1:21; Rev 5:12). All this suggests that a sacrificial appraisal of the life and death of Jesus was a feature of early Christian tradition right from the very beginning of the movement. Hebrews stands out, however, both in terms of the pervasiveness of its sacrificial appraisal (1:3; 7:26–27;

8:3; 9:26–28; 10:11–12) and especially for its own highly distinctive handling of this traditional theme.

PRIESTS AS MEDIATOR FIGURES

The institution and office of the priesthood would have been familiar to a pagan, as well as a Jewish audience. In the Greco-Roman world, priests were a recognizable sight at the many religious festivals that filled the calendars of major urban centers. Such pagan priests engaged in a variety of roles. They oversaw the maintenance of temples, conducted sacrifices, engaged in divination, and interpreted signs and oracles.[4] In a culture, moreover, where the boundary between the political and religious realms was a fluid one, priests were tasked with the responsibility of safeguarding the well-being of the city and its citizenry by properly honoring the divine realm. As we have already seen, the bulk of the persecution experienced by early Christ followers owed to their implicit refusal to honor the traditional gods. By not taking part in the myriad forms of religious pageantry that punctuated much of daily life in a Greco-Roman city, pagan converts risked being labelled as dangerous deviants.

In the ancient Jewish context, Jewish priests likewise performed a variety of functions. They took on the role of teachers and interpreters of the law; assessed and ruled on instances of purity and impurity; looked to discern the will of God; and supported and supervised the complex sacrificial apparatus of the great temple in Jerusalem. During the time of the public ministry of Jesus the chief priests descended from aristocratic families shouldered important administrative responsibilities (see Mark 14:53). One of the

4. See Alan C. Mitchell, *Hebrews*, Sacra Pagina Series 13 (Collegeville, MN: Liturgical Press, 2007), 76.

primary responsibilities of the Jewish high priest was to advocate for the interests of the Jewish people before the Roman imperial authorities (see John 11:48). As was the case with pagan priests, Jewish priests followed stringent protocols in preparation for serving at the altar or sanctuary. This was especially true of the Jewish high priest for whom added requirements were stipulated in the law. These included more stringent marriage requirements, stricter purity regulations, and even specially prescribed clothing.

JEWISH SACRIFICE

It is important to emphasize that not every sacrifice was designed to deal expressly with the problem of sin or transgression. For example, the communion or thanksgiving sacrifice mentioned in Leviticus 7:11–16 consisted of an animal and grain offering that was offered up as a voluntary gift to God. Neither the language of cleansing, nor atonement, nor forgiveness is mentioned at all in the description of this kind of sacrifice. The understanding of sacrifice that we see in Hebrews, therefore, is selective and was influenced by the principal place that the event of the death of Jesus held in early Christian proclamation.

The essential role of a priest, whether pagan or Jewish, was to serve as a mediator between the divine realm and humankind. The priest's role as a mediator implied nothing less than privileged access to the divine. In the case of the Jewish high priest, since only he alone could enter the innermost part of the sanctuary on the annual Day of Atonement, he was thought to have the closest possible access and proximity to God. According to Hebrews, this privileged mediatorial role has now definitively been fulfilled by God's Son (9:15), about whom the author declares,

> Therefore, it was necessary for the copies of the heavenly things to be purified by these rites, but the heavenly things themselves by better sacrifices than these. For Christ did not enter a sanctuary made by hands, a copy of the true one, but heaven itself, that he might now appear before God on our behalf. Not that he might offer himself repeatedly as the high priest enters each year into the sanctuary with blood that is not his own; if that were so, he would have had to suffer repeatedly from the foundation of the world. But now once for all he has appeared at the end of the ages to take away sin by his sacrifice. (9:23–26)

The language Hebrews employs in this passage to describe Christ appearing before God on behalf of the community is the language of mediation. With these preliminary observations in place on the basic meaning of the concepts of sacrifice, atonement, and mediation, we turn now to the description of the priestly Christology of Hebrews.

A SUPERIOR MEDIATOR (HEB 1:1–14)

The first stage in the development of the priestly Christology of Hebrews overlaps with the opening verses of the letter and extends through the close of chapter 2. It is there where we see the first explicit reference to the theme of the high priesthood of Jesus (2:17). Within this broader unit, Hebrews 1:1–14 constitutes what many have called the *exordium* of the letter. The latter is a technical term signifying the formal introduction of an ancient speech. Comparable to how a modern-day speaker might "warm up" an audience by telling a joke or sharing an anecdote, such formal introductions enabled audiences to anticipate the topics to be treated in more detail in the main body of an ancient speech. The exordium was also the place where the speaker—in this case, the anonymous author of Hebrews—would try to make a good first impression, thereby securing a supportive hearing from the audience. Judging by the elevated literary style of the opening verses of Hebrews, the first hearers of the letter would have been impressed by the author's elegant handling of the Greek language, scriptural knowledge base, and deft ability to weave disparate passages of Scripture into surprising patterns of meaning.

HEBREWS 1:1–14: THE EXORDIUM

1:1–4 *The Son as mediator and revealer of God*
1:5–7 *The Son's superiority to the angels*
1:8–14 *The divine status of the Son*

One of the principal themes announced in the exordium concerns the definitive mediatorial role of the Son:

> In times past, God spoke in partial and various ways to our ancestors through the prophets; in these last days, he spoke to us through a son, whom he made heir of all things and through whom he created the universe,
>
> who is the refulgence of his glory,
> the very imprint of his being,
> and who sustains all things by his mighty word.
> (1:1–3a)

Here in the opening lines of the letter, Hebrews employs the metaphor of human speech to articulate the faith commitment that the life, death, and resurrection of Jesus has inaugurated a new age. Much like human speech discloses the interior thoughts of a speaker, Hebrews depicts the Son as the speech that definitively reveals all that God is (1:3a). The opening lines of Hebrews strikingly resemble the first verses of the Gospel of John. There, too, we meet a similar metaphorical usage of divine speech:

> In the beginning was the Word,
> and the Word was with God,
> and the Word was God. (John 1:1)

Both Hebrews and the Fourth Gospel open with unmistakable claims affirming the divine status of the Son.

CHRISTOLOGY IN THE EARLY CHURCH

One of the most pressing issues that confronted Church leaders in the fourth century concerned the question of whether the Son was to be understood as being fully equal to the Father or merely like the Father. Proponents of both views could find passages to support either position. The fourth-century theologian Athanasius advocated for the claim that the Father and Son share the same divine nature or essence. Athanasius found the exordium of Hebrews useful for proving what he understood to be the true assessment of how the Son relates to the Father. The text below comes from Athanasius's *Orations Against the Arians*:

> [The Son] is the Wisdom and Word of the Father, by whom and through whom he creates and makes all things. He is the Father's reflection *[apaugasma*, Heb 1:3] by whom he enlightens all things and is revealed to whomever he wishes. This is the one who is the

> Father's exact imprint [*charaktēr*, Heb 1:3] and image, by which he is contemplated and known, since he and the Father are one [John 10:30]. Indeed, the one who looks at him looks also at the Father [cf. John 14:9]. This is the one who is Christ by whom all things have been redeemed and who has worked out again the new creation [cf. 2 Cor 5:17]. [Translation by Rowan A. Greer]

Hebrews' use of the metaphor of speaking is a fitting one. Not only does it effectively complement the homiletic quality of Hebrews noted above but it also conveys that Christ's status as the definitive mediator between God and humanity flows from a relationship of eternal intimacy between the Son and Father. At the same time, while Hebrews insists that God has spoken genuinely in the past, the author equally affirms that the revelation spoken in the Son surpasses all prior manifestations of God's speech (1:1–2).

The conceptual roots of these opening lines of Hebrews lie deeply in the intellectual soil of the Jewish Wisdom tradition. Attested in a broad range of biblical and extrabiblical texts, this tradition portrays the figure of Wisdom (*Sophia*) as the eternal, personal attribute of God that informs and gives meaning to all reality. As an attribute of God, Wisdom is portrayed as mediating to the visible, created world, the invisible, transcendent presence of the divine:

> For Wisdom is mobile beyond all motion....
> she is a breath of the might of God
> and a pure emanation of the glory of the
>   Almighty;
> therefore nothing defiled can enter into her.
> For she is the reflection of eternal light,

> the spotless mirror of the power of God,
> the image of his goodness. (Wis 7:24–26)

Just as Wisdom reflects the "eternal light" of God's presence, so, too, the exordium of Hebrews portrays the Son as the "radiance" of the glory of God and "the very imprint" of all that God is (1:3a). Likewise, the emphasis Hebrews places on the personal agency of the Son involved in summoning the cosmos into being (1:2) echoes the portrayal of Wisdom found in yet another wisdom text, the Book of Proverbs:

> The LORD begot me, the beginning of his works,
> the forerunner of his deeds of long ago....
> When he established the heavens, there was I....
> When he fixed the foundations of earth,
> then was I beside him as an artisan. (Prov 8:22–30)

Such parallels show how readily the author of Hebrews embraces the terminology associated with the Jewish Wisdom tradition to communicate the audience's deepest commitments concerning the intimate relationship that exists between the Son and the Father. At the same time, Hebrews intensifies the personal aspect attaching to the figure of Wisdom by drawing its audience's attention to the concrete, physical presence of the Son at the right hand of God (1:3c). As a result of this intensification, Hebrews declares something new: the Son who brought all things into existence, and who reveals the glory and impression of the divine presence in the fullest possible sense, is the same Son who came into the world to participate fully in the flesh and blood existence that characterizes humanity (2:14).

JEWISH WISDOM TRADITION

Notable examples of the Wisdom tradition are found in such Jewish biblical texts as the Book of Proverbs, and deuterocanonical texts such as the Wisdom of Solomon, and the Book of Sirach (also known as the Wisdom of Ben Sira). These writings portray Wisdom as eternal (Prov 8:22); involved in the creation and fashioning of the cosmos (Prov 8:26; Sir 24:4–5); and as the embodiment or reflection of all that God is (Wis 7:24–26). Other texts build on these affirmations by linking Wisdom with virtuous action (Wis 8:4–7); with the people of Israel (Sir 24:8); and with the Jewish law or Torah (Sir 24:23). Clear examples of the application of Jewish Wisdom categories to Christ are visible in other New Testament texts besides Hebrews. The most notable are John 1:1–3 and Colossians 1:15–17.

Following closely upon the majestic opening of Hebrews is the main body of the exordium (1:5–14). This section consists of a chain of quotations taken from the Jewish Scriptures and has been selected to set up a comparison between Christ and the figure of the angels (1:5–13). Altogether there are seven of these quotations (1:5a; 1:5b; 1:6; 1:7; 1:8–9; 1:10; 1:13). Several of them (1:5, 13) appear in other New Testament writings, testifying to their evident popularity within the larger Christian tradition. This is particularly true of the first two quotations that Hebrews pairs closely together:

> For to which of the angels did God ever say: "You are my Son; this day I have begotten you"? Or again: "I will be a father to him, and he shall be a son to me"? (1:5)

Located at the beginning of the chain are two quotations taken from Psalm 2:8 and 2 Samuel 7:14, respectively. Both passages already had a lengthy history of being interpreted by early Christ followers as prophecies confirming the royal status of Jesus (see Mark 1:11; Matt 3:17; Luke 1:32–33; 3:22–23). By having these two quotations follow at once after the verse that reads, "For to which of the angels did God ever say" (1:5a), Hebrews depicts God as a speaker who, in the very words of Scripture, personally addresses the Son.

Here we meet with a wonderful example of Hebrews engaging the imagination of its audience in an emotionally powerful way. Through a creative wedding of the visual and the auditory, Hebrews invites the community to enter imaginatively into the heavenly sanctuary. Once there, they are privileged to overhear the Father welcoming the Son into heaven after the tragic event of the crucifixion (1:3d). From this point, on through the rest of the exordium (1:5–14), the audience eavesdrops on a conversation in which God is heard addressing two separate dialogue partners: the Son (1:5, 8–9, 10–13) and the angels (1:6, 7). On balance, however, it turns out that God has much more to say to the Son!

The author's stated purpose in setting up this comparison is to show the superiority of the Son to the angels (see 1:4). Still, we might wonder why Hebrews considers it important to draw such a comparison in the first place. Would it not have been obvious to Hebrews' audience that God's Son is superior to the angels? A possible answer to that question may rest in the conceptual background to the letter. Speculation over the mediatorial role of angels was quite common for the period in which Hebrews was written. Most persons who lived in the ancient world took for granted that presences and powers of various kinds populated the cosmos and could influence human behavior. This explains one reason why narratives about angelic figures appear so often throughout the Bible, where they function as ambassadors from the divine realm. In their capacity as ambassadors, angels are depicted as performing a variety of mediating functions, ranging from delivering messages from God (see Gen 18:1–14; Matt 1:20; Luke 1:11–17); providing interpretations of events (Mark 16:6; Rev 7:13–17); and even lavishing protection and guidance upon the community (see Exod 23:20–23; Matt 2:13). In addition, both biblical and extrabiblical sources envision angelic figures occupying a privileged place of physical proximity to the divine (e.g., Ezek 1:4–28; Rev 4:1–6; 7:1–2). As we will see in a moment, this last point has relevance for understanding key elements of Hebrews' Christology.

Immersed in these contemporary beliefs, the author of Hebrews reminds the audience that not even admittedly glorious creatures such as angels are superior to the Son, who alone is seated at the right hand of God (1:4, 14). While sharing the belief that angels can serve as ambassadors of God (1:14), the author nonetheless portrays the Son alone as mediating the definitive speech of God, as well as embodying the radiance and imprint of God's essential being (1:1–3a). According to Hebrews, then, the Son's intimate relationship to God transcends mere proximity to the divine and instead touches on identity with the divine. This emphasis on the divine status of the Son will be a consistent theme proclaimed throughout the sermon, especially in those passages where Hebrews compares the eternal status of Christ's high priesthood with the priesthood of merely human high priests (7:15, 23).

It should not be surprising, therefore, that one of the quotations in the scriptural chain of citations envisions God calling upon the angels to worship the Son (1:6). This emphasis on the divine status of Christ is driven home for the audience in the final instances of dialogue addressed by God to the Son:

Your throne, O God, stands forever and ever;
and a righteous scepter is the scepter of your kingdom.
You loved justice and hated wickedness;
therefore God, your God, anointed you
with the oil of gladness above your companions. (1:8–9)

At the beginning, O Lord, you established the earth,
and the heavens are the works of your hands.
They will perish, but you remain;
and they will all grow old like a garment.
You will roll them up like a cloak,
and like a garment they will be changed.
But you are the same, and your years will have no end. (1:10–12)

Once again, a collection of quotations is taken from the Psalms; in this instance, Psalm 45:7–8 and 102:26–28. In its original context as either a court or temple poem, Psalm 45 conferred the honorific title of God upon the anointed Jewish king, the royal figure who uniquely represented the will of God on earth. By replacing the anonymous poet behind Psalm 45 with God, Hebrews boldly declares that what was said metaphorically of the Jewish king is now said literally of the Son: "Your throne, O God, stands forever and ever" (1:8a).

THE MEDIATORIAL ROLE OF THE JEWISH PRIEST

The essential role of the Jewish priest as a mediator is beautifully illustrated in this passage taken from the Book of

Exodus in which God is portrayed as addressing Moses with this promise:

> There, at the altar, I will meet the Israelites; hence, it will be made sacred by my glory. Thus, I will consecrate the tent of meeting and the altar, just as I also consecrate Aaron and his sons to be my priests. I will dwell in the midst of the Israelites and will be their God. They shall know that I, the LORD, am their God who brought them out of the land of Egypt, so that I, the LORD, their God, might dwell among them. (Exod 29:43–46)

Emphasized throughout this passage is the assurance that the God of Israel will draw near to the people and dwell among them. Both the altar for sacrifice, and the priests consecrated to serve at the altar, are portrayed as the vehicles through which the encounter with God is to occur. Stated another way, Aaron and his sons appear in this passage as the unique mediators of the encounter between the God of Israel and the Israelites. According to Hebrews, however, it is the Son who now mediates (7:25; 8:6, 15), consecrates (9:13–14; 10:10), and makes it truly possible for God to dwell in the hearts and minds of the faithful (10:19–22).

Hebrews's use of an extended quotation from Psalm 102 presents an even more explicit appraisal of the divine status of the Son. In its original context, Psalm 102 celebrated the transcendent, eternal status of the God of Israel, as well as the lordship of the God of Israel over all creation. By presenting none other than God as the speaker of the psalm, Hebrews empowers the audience to hear these words anew: the same qualities of transcendence and eternity that belong properly to God are now seen to apply also to the Son. And as if to emphasize for one final time that the Son is the definitive mediator of God, Hebrews once more employs the dramatic visual image of the Son's session at the right hand of God by quoting from Psalm 110:1: "But to which of the angels has he ever said, 'Sit at my right hand until I make your enemies your footstool'?" (Heb 1:13).

A HIGH PRIEST WHO DRAWS NEAR (HEB 2:1–18)

If the exordium of Hebrews focuses on the theme of the exalted heavenly status of Christ, the material that follows it (2:1–18) turns its attention instead to the theme of the humanity of Christ. There Hebrews builds further upon the motif by designating Jesus a high priest who makes possible the expiation of sins (2:17–18). This section also introduces broader theological themes that will be developed more fully in later sections of the letter. Included among these themes are the solicitude and compassion that Christ shows on behalf of humanity (2:16), as well as the Son's commitment to the role of fulfilling the will of God concerning the salvation of humanity (2:10).

HEBREWS 2:1–18

2:1–4 *Words of warning to the community*
2:5–9 *Jesus as humanity's representative*
2:10–13 *The Son in solidarity with humanity*
2:14–18 *Victory over death: the incarnation of the Son*

This new section of the letter opens with a warning to the community on the importance of attending to the implications of the majestic portrayal of Christ set up by the exordium. Having shown that Christ is both the definitive revelation of God and is superior to the angels, Hebrews now urges the community not to neglect the greatness of the salvation bestowed on them (2:1–4). The material that follows in verses 5 through 9 clarifies for the audience the substance of this great salvation. Hebrews emphasizes the profound human-centeredness of salvation; its substance is nothing less than humankind's inheritance of a heavenly age-to-come, the same heavenly realm where the Son presently reigns with God. And, in a surprising twist on the topic of the angels, Hebrews affirms that human beings were forever destined to be heirs to this coming age (1:14) and that this heavenly destiny belongs expressly to humanity rather than to the angels (2:5).

Holding a place of prominence in this section is Psalm 8, which the author interprets as a disclosure of the divine intention to bring all humanity to eschatological glory through the agency of the Son (2:10). In its original setting in the Jewish Scriptures, Psalm 8 celebrated the exalted and privileged stature of humankind as compared with the rest of creation:

> What is [a human being] that you are mindful of
> him,
> or the son of man that you care for him?
> You made him a little while lower than the
> angels;
> you crowned him with glory and honor,
> subjecting all things under his feet. (Heb 2:6–8)

Scripture bears a surplus of meaning that allows for its appropriation in different contexts. Hebrews reenvisions the deeper meaning of this psalm by seeing the human being Jesus as the true focus of the psalm's mention of "humankind" [*anthrōpos*] (2:6). Hebrews thus envisions Jesus as the representative human being who sums up all that humanity is destined to share in fulfillment of the original vision of the psalm.

Guided by this christological reading of the psalm, Hebrews interprets Psalm 8's mention of the lowering of humanity beneath the angels as a prophecy that points to the suffering and death of Jesus during his historical ministry (2:9). Guided by the same conviction that the psalm points to Jesus, Hebrews interprets the psalm's declaration concerning the crowning of humankind with glory and honor as an allusion to the future exaltation of Jesus (2:9). In this way, the audience is led to see that Jesus has already fulfilled in himself the destined goal for all humanity who follow in his steps. We may not go too far afield in saying that Hebrews views Jesus as the maturity of the human race, much like Paul does (compare 1 Cor 15:45–49).

While the author of Hebrews is aware that eschatological glory remains for now an unseen reality (2:8), the end-time event of the "subjecting of all things" (2:8) is nonetheless assured because Jesus, as humankind's representative, has already entered the presence of God on behalf of humanity. Jesus thereby makes possible the future subjection of all things to human beings (2:8). In the meantime, echoing the earlier invitation to the audience to enter imaginatively into heaven to behold Jesus's exaltation, Hebrews declares that the community sees this promise already fulfilled in the risen Jesus, who lives forever in the presence of God's glory.

PERFECTION THROUGH SUFFERING (HEB 2:10)

Having set up the representative role of Jesus through a christological reading of Psalm 8, Hebrews continues to highlight the precise way in which the human Jesus makes the promise of salvation possible. The author reminds the audience that salvation has become a possibility not despite Jesus's experiences of suffering and death, but precisely through such traumatic experiences: "For it was fitting that he, for whom and through whom all things exist, in bringing many children to glory, should make the leader to their salvation perfect through suffering" (2:10). While Hebrews is not the only New Testament text that uses the language of perfection (see John 4:34; 5:36; 19:30), the way in which Hebrews applies this terminology directly to the person of Jesus is unique. Hebrews portrays Jesus as being "perfected" no less than three times in the letter (2:10; 5:9; 7:28), with the first of these occurrences appearing in the section presently under analysis (2:10). The root meaning of the Greek word for perfection connotes the idea of wholeness or completion (*teleioō*). Often, however, the context of this perfection terminology shapes the precise meaning of the wholeness or completion that is in view. But this definition at once raises the question: In what sense could Jesus have been made whole or complete? This question only becomes sharper when we consider later passages in the letter that declare that the high priest Jesus was not in any way deficient or lacking in excellent qualities (see 4:15; 7:26).

The answer to this question rests once more in Hebrews' interpretation of Psalm 8. Hebrews has already declared that humanity's destiny of glory and honor has been fulfilled in the life and death of the human Jesus. Because the Son has tasted death on behalf of humanity (2:9), Jesus has been exalted into God's presence where he now lives forever crowned with glory and honor (2:9). But as Hebrews goes on to show in the following verse, "glory" is also the salvific destiny toward which God is leading all of humanity in and through Jesus, who as humanity's representative is also their pioneer, the first human being to experience glory understood as complete access to God. If we ask what is the substance of this glory, the answer seems already to have been given in the opening chapter of Hebrews. Glory is nothing less than entrance into God's presence. According to the grand vision of Hebrews, the human Jesus, as humanity's representative, was the first to enter God's presence when God raised Jesus from the dead (10:12; 13:20). The same destiny of glory understood as access to God awaits all the faithful as well (1:14; 2:5). To claim that Jesus has been perfected, then, is Hebrews' way of affirming that the human Jesus was made whole or complete when he was raised from the dead and exalted into God's presence where he now sits at God's right hand (1:3).

Jesus's perfection, then, entails his exaltation. Yet this is not all that it entails. Hebrews also declares that Jesus was perfected through his own personal experience of suffering and death (2:9–10; 5:8–9). What Hebrews means is that Jesus's coming to completion through suffering and death revealed the ultimate depths of Jesus's commitment to draw near to humanity. According to Hebrews, the fittingness or appropriateness of the sufferings that led to Jesus tasting death (2:9) reveals that Jesus is not only humanity's representative, but the one who chose in faithfulness to God's will to be in complete solidarity with human beings (2:11–13). Only by immersing himself completely into all that it entailed to be human—even to the point of experiencing suffering and death—could God's Son truly experience concretely what it meant to be in complete solidarity with the siblings that make up humankind.

SOLIDARITY WITH HUMANITY (HEB 2:14–18)

As one who is in perfect solidarity with the community, Jesus is the community's leader (*archēgon*) who is "not ashamed to call" the individual members of this community his brothers and sisters (2:10–11). Jesus is the leader who has entered human existence not to "help angels but rather the descendants of Abraham" (2:16). Hebrews is working, therefore, with an understanding of perfection that, when applied to Jesus, implies a double assessment: Jesus is perfected in the sense that he has been exalted into heaven, but the very basis of that exaltation stems from the Son's prior commitment to draw near to humanity in the most radical of ways possible, by becoming one of them (2:14).

This movement in the argument of Hebrews leading from the affirmation of Jesus's representative status to the claim about the Son's perfect solidarity with humankind prepares the way for the event that has so far only been implicit in the author's argument, namely, the incarnation where the Son partakes of flesh-and-blood human existence:

> Now since the children share in blood and flesh, he likewise shared in them, that through death he might destroy the one who has the power of death, that is, the devil, and free those who through fear of death had been subject to slavery all their life. Surely he did not help angels but rather the descendants of Abraham; and therefore, he had to become like his brothers [and sisters] in every way, that he might be a merciful and faithful high priest before God to expiate the sins of the people. Because he himself was tested through what he suffered, he is able to help those who are being tested. (2:14–18)

Hebrews insists in the strongest possible terms that the Son took part fully in embodied human existence, with all the limitations and vulnerability that go with flesh and blood existence. Hebrews has already affirmed that Jesus tasted death (2:9); now the audience is told that, through death,

Jesus has conquered the one who held the power of death, namely Satan (2:14).

The original audience for Hebrews would have received the message that Christ had liberated them from the tyranny of the fear of death with profound gratitude (2:14). It may be difficult for readers today to appreciate just how unrelenting the fear of death could be for most ordinary persons in antiquity. During the period of the early Roman Empire infant mortality rates were horrifically high and life expectancy for adults was well below the threshold of what today we would consider to constitute the very young. By assuring the community that Jesus has liberated them from life-long slavery to the "fear of death" (2:15), Hebrews effectively emphasizes the present dimension of salvation. Although entrance into God's glory is still a future inheritance reserved for the age to come (1:14; 2:5, 10), liberation from the psychological anxiety attending the concrete frailty of human existence is available now to the members of this community.

As is the case with the four Gospels and several of the letters of Paul, Hebrews also appears to be familiar with early traditions that saw the power of the kingdom embodied by Jesus as conquering the personalized source of evil: Satan or the devil (2:14). Hebrews is less interested, however, in exploring the details of the mythological struggle between good and evil than with emphasizing what Jesus's triumph over the tyrannical power of death implies about the kind of a high priest Jesus is. Looking on the human community as siblings (2:12), indeed his very children (2:13), the Son is committed to assuming their flesh and blood existence (2:14). What this implies, in turn, is that the Son fully enters into the myriad experiences that accompany human existence. These include physical suffering (2:10) as well as the fear of death that is a part of embodied existence (5:7).

According to the author of Hebrews, Jesus's immersion in the flesh and blood existence of humanity is necessary (2:17) if the Son is to qualify completely as a "merciful and faithful high priest" (2:17). For only one who has endured the testing that goes with embodied existence is qualified to aid to those who are similarly tested (2:18).

According to Hebrews, then, Jesus is a special kind of high priest, one whose character is epitomized by the qualities of mercy and faithfulness gained by experience. As has been suggested by Luke Timothy Johnson, it is quite possible that the combination of the qualities of mercy and faithfulness mentioned in 2:17 are meant to recall the description of God's character as it appears in such texts as Exodus 34:5–6, where God is described as graceful and abounding in love and fidelity (faithfulness).[5] As applied to Jesus, this description not only alludes once more to the Son's divine nature, but just as importantly to the Son's commitment to give expression to that divine love in the most concrete and vulnerable of ways.

ADAM AND EVE AS CHILDREN

The idea that Christ represents the maturity or perfection of humanity is powerfully and poetically expressed by Irenaeus of Lyons:

> So also it was possible for God Himself to have made man perfect from the first, but man could not receive this [perfection], being as yet an infant. And for this cause our Lord, in these last times, when He had summed up all things into Himself, came to us, not as

5. Luke Timothy Johnson, *Hebrews: A Commentary, New Testament Library* (Louisville, KY: Westminster John Knox, 2006), 104.

> He might have come, but as we were capable of beholding him. He might easily have come to us in His immortal glory, but in that case we could never have endured the greatness of the glory; and therefore it was that He, who was the perfect bread of the Father, offered Himself to us as milk, [because we were] as infants. (*Against Heresies* 4.38.1)

Irenaeus's description of the first human beings as children is inspired by a passage taken from the Letter to the Ephesians: "In all wisdom and insight, he has made known to us the mystery of his will in accord with his favor that he set forth in him as a plan for the fullness of times, to sum up all things in Christ, in heaven and on earth" (Eph 1:8–10). It was from this passage that Irenaeus developed his distinctive concept of recapitulation. The incarnation of the Son has made it possible for human beings to grow and mature into the full flowering of the image of God. That process of maturity was interrupted by the fall in Eden but is now empowered once more to begin afresh as a result of the Christ event.

Chapter Three

Jesus, the Faithful High Priest

At the heart of the priestly Christology of Hebrews is the declaration that Jesus is the divine mediator who, within a heavenly sanctuary, offers the sacrifice of his own self to God (9:15–27). Christ is also the merciful and faithful high priest (2:17) who took part fully in embodied human existence (2:14), even to the limit of willingly embracing suffering (2:10, 18) and death (2:9) in his role as the representative of humanity (2:8–9). This embodied commitment is integral, moreover, to what it means to say that Jesus was perfected (2:10). Jesus was perfected in the sense that he became qualified to become a high priest. Such priestly qualification involves two emphases held in creative tension. On the one hand, Hebrews unites the priestly qualification of Christ to the heavenly exaltation of the Son following the events of the suffering and death of Jesus (2:9). On the other hand, by understanding the testing of Jesus as part of a larger process of priestly qualification, Hebrews weds the theme of perfection to the human career of God's Son: "For it was fitting that he, for whom and through whom all things exist, in bringing many children to glory, should make the leader of their salvation perfect through suffering" (2:10; 5:8–9). For Hebrews, then, Jesus's qualification to become a high priest derives both from his complete solidarity with humanity and the event of his exaltation to heaven. Taken together, both emphases constitute what it means to say that God's Son was perfected.

The author concludes this first stage in the development of Hebrews' priestly Christology by declaring that the qualities of mercy and faithfulness embodied in the human career of Christ are tied somehow to the goal of the purification of sins (2:17). For the moment, Hebrews merely asserts this claim, leaving the specifics of the connection unexplained. The next stage in the development of Hebrews' priestly Christology clarifies this connection by focusing on Jesus's human response of faithfulness before God (5:7–8). By plumbing the depths of all that complete obedience to God entailed, Jesus learned what it meant to embody fully, for the first time, a human life that was marked by sinlessness (4:15; 5:8). In turn, Jesus's embodiment of such a life resulted in the possibility for other humans to live lives purified from sins as well. Put another way, while Jesus's solidarity with humanity was all-encompassing, it was at the same time thoroughly unique both in its manifestation and effects. In his role as humanity's representative, Jesus supplies the first example of a human life lived in complete obedience to God. As a reward for embodying such a life, God hears Jesus (5:7), exalting "the leader and perfector of faith" (12:2) to new life (12:2). It was this response of faithfulness, according to Hebrews, that led not only to Jesus's glorification in heaven but also to the purification from sins (1:3c; 2:18; 9:26; 10:19–22). By overturning the power of sin, Jesus inaugurated, according to Hebrews, a new way of access to God (4:16).

THE GREATER GLORY OF THE SON (HEB 3:1–6)

Hebrews begins this new stage in its argument by once again drawing the audience's attention to the gift of salvation they have received:

> Therefore, holy "brothers [and sisters]," sharing in a heavenly calling, reflect on Jesus, the apostle and high priest of our confession, who was faithful to the one who appointed him, just as Moses "was faithful in [all] his house." (3:1–2)

Although chapter 3 begins a new phase in the explication of Hebrews' priestly Christology with the mention of the figure of Moses, this new section also revisits several themes and literary strategies from earlier in the letter (2:1–18). For example, by affirming the community's participation in a "heavenly calling" (3:1), Hebrews echoes earlier assurances about the promise of a heavenly destiny awaiting the faithful (1:14; 2:5). The employment of familiar literary techniques also appears: an affinity for connecting theological exposition to exhortation (3:1, 6); the use of literary comparison to advance christological claims (3:2–5); the recurrence of the theme of Jesus's faithfulness (3:2). At the same, these are all taken up and developed in new ways. For example, whereas the exhortations that appear earlier in the letter (2:1–4) are brief and encouraging in tone, those found in this section are lengthier and more serious; while the comparisons put on display in the first two chapters of Hebrews emphasized the unequal relationship between the Son and the angels, this new section concentrates on the comparison between Jesus and Moses, as well as the comparison between Jesus and the human high priest; finally, whereas the topic of Jesus's faithfulness was attached previously to the theme of the Son's commitment to humanity demonstrated by the incarnation (2:14), far greater emphasis is given in this new section to the response of faithfulness that the human Jesus expressed directly before God (5:7–8).

Returning to the text, we see that Hebrews addresses an appeal to the community to consider that Jesus—whom the author now describes as both apostle and high priest (3:1)—was "faithful" [*piston*] to the one who appointed him (3:2). Following this appeal, Hebrews next introduces a comparison between Jesus and the figure of Moses, the great Jewish prophet and hero of the exodus story:

> Therefore, holy "brothers [and sisters]," sharing in a heavenly calling, reflect on Jesus, the apostle and high priest of our confession, who was faithful to the one who appointed him, just as Moses was "faithful in [all] his house." But [Jesus] is worthy of more "glory" than Moses, as the founder of a house has more "honor" than the house itself. Every house is founded by someone, but the founder of all is God. Moses was "faithful in all his house" as a "servant" to testify to what would be spoken, but Christ was faithful as a son placed over his house. We are his house, if [only] we hold fast to our confidence and pride in our hope. (3:1–6)

Only here in the New Testament is Jesus given the title of apostle, a title employed elsewhere in the New Testament to refer to the divinely commissioned appointment of one who preaches the gospel (see Luke 6:13; Matt 28:19; Rom 16:7; Gal 1:1, 15–17). Like the title of high priest, this new title for Jesus challenges the audience to think about him in a new way. While initially it might appear odd that a title reserved for followers of Jesus is given to Jesus himself, its application begins to make more sense as a result of the deeper implications to be drawn from the comparison between the figures of Jesus and Moses.

Both in the Jewish Scriptures as well as in later Jewish tradition, Moses was remembered as the uniquely authorized prophet of God; Moses was celebrated, in other words, precisely as a mediator. It was Moses whom the God of Israel charged to lead the Israelites out of their captivity in Egypt for the purpose of establishing a covenant relationship with them (Exod 3:1–10). It was likewise through the agency of Moses that God supplied sustenance to the famished and thirsty Israelites in the form of manna and water during their journey in the wilderness (Exod 16:4–5; 17:1:7). It was specifically through the mediation of Moses that the God of Israel gave the law to the people (Exod 20:1 – 23:19). Moreover, in this same law, Moses is described as a prophet who held a special intimacy with God; indeed, in the Jewish Scriptures, Moses alone is portrayed as one with whom the Lord spoke "face to face" (Exod 33:11). The Jewish Scriptures refer to Moses as someone uniquely given a glimpse of the divine presence (Exod 33:17–23).

Examples such as these, which demonstrate the privileged status of Moses in Jewish tradition, help illumine several of Hebrews' statements regarding the exalted status of Jesus. In what may function as an allusion to the mediatorial role of Moses, Hebrews depicts Jesus as the divinely appointed leader (*archēgos*), whose mission is to bring "many children to glory" (2:10). And, in a manner analogous to the liberating role Moses plays in the story of the exodus, Hebrews likewise portrays the Son as a liberator. But the liberation that Hebrews has in view involves deliverance from the existential slavery of the fear of death rather than physical enslavement (2:15).

Given the celebrated status of Moses as God's preeminent mediator in Jewish tradition, as well as the prominent place that Hebrews gives to the mediatorial role of Christ as high priest, it seems logical that Hebrews would wish to compare Jesus favorably with Moses. Such a comparative task is also in keeping with what we have already noted concerning the rhetorical artistry of Hebrews. When public speakers in antiquity wished to emphasize the excellence of a biographical subject, often they would compare that person to a recognized figure whom all could agree bore a reputation for excellence. For a Jewish audience, or for a Gentile audience familiar with Jewish traditions, few figures available for such a comparative task would have been a better choice than that of Moses.

MOSES IN LATER JEWISH TRADITION

The esteem with which Moses was regarded by Jews in antiquity is attested in many postbiblical traditions. Below is one example taken from the writings of the Jewish philosopher Philo of Alexandria, whose vast body of writings includes two major treatises devoted to the life of Moses. For Philo, Moses is something of a superhuman figure, someone who encompasses in his person the four principal virtues of kingship, philosopher, high priest, and prophet:

> But Moses will be seen not only to have displayed all these powers—I mean the genius of the philosopher and the king—in an extraordinary degree at the same time, but three other powers likewise, one of which

> was conversant about legislation, the second about the way of discharging the duties of the high priest and the last about the prophetic office....For I conceive that all these things have fitly been united in him, inasmuch as in accordance with the providential will of God he was both a king and a lawgiver, and a high priest and a prophet, and because in each office he displayed the most eminent wisdom and virtue. (Philo, *Life of Moses*, 2.2)

Echoing the force of the comparison between the Son and the angels in the exordium of Hebrews, the comparison in this new section of the argument conveys that Jesus is superior to Moses. It is important to note, however, the precise terms of the comparison that Hebrews uses. Surprisingly, Hebrews does not underscore the different degrees of faithfulness evinced by Jesus and Moses. Instead, the comparison between these two figures is centered on the relative glory or honor that belongs properly to each (3:2). After declaring that Jesus was "faithful to the one who appointed him," Hebrews adds, "just as Moses was 'faithful in [all] his house.'" But he is worthy of more "glory" than Moses (3:2). Hebrews takes the first part of this quotation from the Book of Numbers, in a passage where Moses is described as occupying an especially honored place among the Lord's prophets:

> If there are prophets among you,
> in visions I reveal myself to them,
> in dream I speak to them;
> Not so with my servant Moses!
> Throughout my house he is worthy of trust.
> (Num 12:6–7)

The "house" in view in this passage from Numbers serves as a metaphor designating the covenant community of Israel. While Hebrews acknowledges that Moses, like Jesus, was "faithful, in all God's house" and therefore deserving of glory or honor—the Greek noun *doxa* carried both meanings—Jesus is said to be deserving of comparatively more glory (3:3). This greater glory flows from his unique status as the divine Son who presides "over God's house" (3:6). By contrast, Moses is identified as "faithful in all [God's] house" (Heb 3:2) "as a servant" (3:5).

Hebrews' identification of Moses as a servant carries with it an honorable assessment of him, since the term *servant* (like *apostle*) envisions someone who obediently follows the will of another. For example, in the Jewish Scriptures, the people of Israel can be spoken of as God's servant (see Isa 42:1; 49:5; 52:13), implying their faithful obedience to God's will. Similarly, each of the four Gospels calls attention to the obedience that Jesus demonstrated in his observance of God's will (see Matt 4:1–10; Mark 14:36; Luke 22:42; John 5:19–30). When one remembers, moreover, that the ancient definition of a "son" signified a dependent who obediently imitated what he saw the father doing, the designation of Jesus as a son similarly carries the connotation of a servant-like status. But, since Hebrews claims that Jesus is superior to Moses, the author invests the title *son* with more than just a servant connotation, especially given the fact that Moses is described as a servant.

Looking to the cultural context of the intended audience of Hebrews may prove helpful here. The social construction of ancient Mediterranean society was rigidly hierarchal (see Col 3:18—4:1). Within an ancient household, the householder's firstborn son would naturally be thought of as having greater social status and honor than a servant. When we consider, therefore, the kinds of associations that an ancient audience might connect with the terms *servant* versus *son*, Hebrews relativizes or lowers the honor rating of Moses in comparison to Jesus.[1] Something similar might pertain to Hebrews' use of the "house" metaphor. In contrast to Moses, who is characterized as one faithful within God's house (3:5), Jesus is the privileged son who lives over the household (understood metaphorically as the renewed people of God). Hebrews further relativizes the greatness of Moses by labeling him a servant whose role is a rather limited one: "to testify to what would be spoken" (3:5). The emphasis here on the faculty of speech recalls the opening verses of Hebrews, where the partial speech of God that was borne witness to by the prophets (1:1) is contrasted with the definitive revelation of God spoken in the person of the Son (1:2).

JESUS THE FAITHFUL ADAM

The prominence that Hebrews attaches to the theme of the faithful obedience of Jesus was already a traditional claim made by the first communities of Christ followers. Here are two Pauline passages that illustrate the theme:

> For if, by the transgression of one person, death came to reign through that one, how much more will those who receive the abundance of grace and of the gift of justification come to reign in life through the one person Jesus Christ... For just as through the disobedience of one person the many were made sinners, so through the obedience of one the many will be made righteous. (Rom 5:17–19)

1. Luke Timothy Johnson, *Hebrews: A Commentary*, *New Testament Library* (Louisville, KY: Westminster John Knox, 2006), 108–11.

> So, too, it is written, "The first [human], Adam, became a living being"; the last Adam a life-giving spirit. But the spiritual was not first; rather the natural and then the spiritual. The first [human] was from the earth, earthly; the second [human], from heaven. As was the earthly one, so also are the earthly, and as is the heavenly one, so also are the heavenly. Just as we have borne the image of the earthly one, we shall also bear the image of the heavenly one. (1 Cor 15:45–49)

Implicit in the comparison between Jesus and Moses is the conviction that Jesus also shares a unique relationship of intimacy with God, an intimacy tantamount to identity. Since the Son is the reflection of God's glory and the imprint of God's substance (1:3a), the glory of the Son must necessarily be greater than the glory that belonged to Moses. While Hebrews does not denigrate the memory of Moses by denying him any glory and honor, the christological commitments that inform Hebrews inevitably lead the author to relativize the praise bestowed upon any figure in comparison with Jesus. This is true whether the comparison involves Moses, high priests, or angels. It appears, then, that the comparison between Moses and Jesus depends more on what the author sees as the relative glory belonging to each figure than it does on their respective responses of faithfulness. This does not mean, however, that Hebrews leaves the theme of faithfulness entirely behind. From this point on in the sermon the theme of the faithfulness of Jesus will increasingly become a central feature of the author's priestly Christology. Hebrews will go on to claim, in fact, that the response of faithfulness shown by Jesus was so unique that it resulted in nothing less than the opening of a "new and living way" of access to God (10:19–20; 4:16).

REPLACEMENT LANGUAGE IN THE LETTER TO THE HEBREWS

The way in which Hebrews ascribes greater glory to Jesus in relation to Moses highlights one of the many ways Hebrews employs sharply comparative language in articulating its Christology. For example, the author appears to relish any opportunity to use the Greek adjective "better" (*kreitton*) to stress the superiority of Christ (see 6:9; 7:7, 19, 22; 8:6; 9:23; 10:34; 11:16, 35, 40; 12:24) or to emphasize the gift of superior access to God as a result of the Christ event (7:19, 22). Since Hebrews makes such claims primarily through a creative reinterpretation of key Jewish concepts like that of sacrifice, covenant, law, and sanctuary, the language sounds quite exclusive.

The contemporary claim that the Christ event serves as a replacement for Jewish institutions and even the covenantal standing of Jews is called supersessionism. Given the abhorrent prevalence today of both anti-Jewish rhetoric as well as frequent physical violence against Jews, it is crucial to examine the exclusive language of Hebrews or of any other New Testament writing in a nuanced way. It seems clear that Hebrews understands Jewish symbols and institutions as finding their full perfection in and through Christ. But it is important to recognize that this understanding is not an objective but a perspectival claim. Early Christ followers (many of whom were Jewish) interpreted the writings of the Jewish Scriptures in new ways and found new meanings there precisely because of their faith experience of the resurrection of Jesus. Although their interpretation was sincere, that does not mean that Jews today should be expected either to see or accept the meanings that the author of Hebrews ascribes to those texts. Contemporary Jews interpret the scriptural narrative and regard Jewish traditions in ways that are authentic to their own varied experiences and perspectives, and this must always be honored and respected.

THE COMMUNITY'S CONFESSION: JESUS, THE FAITHFUL HIGH PRIEST (HEB 4:14–5:10)

After reminding the audience of their confession celebrating Jesus as their divine apostle and high priest (3:1) and affirming the Son's superiority to Moses (3:1–6), Hebrews turns to clarifying the deeper implications of this confession by comparing Jesus for the first time with human high priests:

> Therefore, since we have a great high priest who has passed through the heavens, Jesus, the Son of God, let us hold fast to our confession. For we do not have a high priest who is unable to sympathize with our weaknesses, but one who has similarly been tested in every way, yet without sin. So let us confidently approach the throne of grace to receive mercy and to find grace for timely help. (4:14–16)

This new comparative task opens with the designation of Jesus as a "great high priest who has passed through the heavens" (4:14). The added qualification of the word "great" to Jesus's priesthood hints at the forthcoming comparison with human high priests that will inform much of the author's priestly Christology throughout the remainder of the letter. With the introduction of the striking image of Jesus's movement through the heavens (4:14), Hebrews anticipates a claim that will be developed in chapters 7—10. There the audience will be reminded that, unlike human high priests who conduct their ministry on earth in a humanly constructed sanctuary, Jesus is a heavenly high priest who mediates for the faithful in a heavenly sanctuary (7:18–28; 10:11–12). Before this, however, Hebrews attributes to Jesus, the great high priest, the emotional stance of compassion towards the weaknesses that attend human existence: "For we do not have a high priest who is unable to sympathize with our weaknesses" (4:15). Only Hebrews among the New Testament texts describes Christ with this rare Greek verb *sympathēsai*, expressive of the human emotion of empathy or sympathy (see also 10:34). The description wonderfully complements the solidarity that the Son shares with humanity. By describing the Son as sympathetic or compassionate, Hebrews affirms for the audience that this great high priest "who has passed through the heavens" (4:14) is the same Jesus who took on human flesh and blood in the incarnation and who continues to show abiding empathy for the vulnerabilities that characterize human existence.

This compassionate portrayal of Jesus is likely an echo of the traditional emphasis (found in all four Gospels) on Jesus as a powerful healer. While the Gospel accounts of these healings show signs of creative adaptation, they also reveal an authentic aspect of the public ministry of Jesus. Many of these Gospel miracle accounts include explicit references to the compassion Jesus demonstrated toward the afflicted (see Mark 1:40–45; Luke 7:11–14). Still other episodes from the Gospels illustrate Jesus's compassion in more indirect ways, as in the episode where Jesus weeps for his friend Lazarus, who has recently died (John 11:32–36), or when Jesus is considerate enough to be aware that the twelve-year-old girl whom he has raised needs something to eat (Mark 5:43). Heir to such traditional memories, Hebrews creatively associates them with the dynamic image of Jesus passing through the heavens as a result of his exaltation. In doing so, Hebrews reminds the audience that even now in his exalted resurrected life Jesus is still the compassionate and sympathetic Savior that he was during his public ministry. Hebrews thus takes this insight about the compassionate character of Jesus and develops it in such a way that it serves to complement the pastoral purposes of the letter. Once again, we see Hebrews preserving the christological tension between the image of the risen Jesus reigning in heaven with the assurance that the risen Jesus continues to give merciful aid to all who look to him as their great high priest (4:16; 2:18).

Hebrews endeavors, however, to impress upon the audience that such empathy and compassion is hard won, in the sense that it has for its foundation the personal testing that the Son experienced during his human career. While Hebrews frequently refers to the testing that the human Jesus endured (4:15; 5:7; 12:3), perhaps the most explicit and powerful portrait of such testing is seen in the following passage:

> In the days when he was in the flesh, he offered prayers and supplications with loud cries and tears to the one who was able to save him from death, and he was heard because of his reverence. Son though he was, he learned obedience from what he suffered, and when he was made perfect, he became the source of eternal salvation for all who obey him, declared by God high priest according to the order of Melchizedek. (5:7–10)

We glimpse in this passage another traditional memory that envisions the faithful obedience Jesus displayed before God. In the Letter to the Philippians, for instance, Paul portrays Christ as one who, "though he was in the form of God...emptied himself...[and], taking the form of a slave... [became] obedient to death, even death on a cross" (Phil 2:6–8). Another example of the same traditional memory concerning the exemplary obedience of Jesus is preserved in the Gospel of Mark (14:32–42). Momentarily bending under the distressing prospect of facing his death, Jesus eventually aligns his will with that of the will of the Father (Mark 14:33–36). Hebrews likewise associates the memory of Jesus's prayer in Gethsemane with an even more vivid manifestation of Jesus's distress: "he offered prayers and supplications with loud cries and tears to the one who was able to save him from death" (5:7). Hebrews' unique contribution to the tradition concerning Jesus's faithfulness is twofold: First, Hebrews explicitly envisions Jesus's embodied obedience expressed in his physical cries and tears as a sacrificial offering to God (5:7). That is, the faithfulness shown by Jesus witnesses to the Son's deeply personal gift to the Father. Indeed, the Greek verb translated above as "offered" (5:7) is the same Greek verb used to describe what the human high priest is mandated to offer before God: "Every high priest is taken from among men and made their representative before God, to offer gifts and sacrifices for sins" (5:1). Jesus, whom we already know is the representative human being in fulfillment of Psalm 8, offers to God not just any gift, but the gift of his own person, symbolized in his prayerful cries and tears:

> But this one offered one sacrifice for sins, and took his seat forever at the right hand of God; now he waits until his enemies are made his footstool. For by one offering he has made perfect forever those who are being consecrated. (10:12–14)

The second contribution Hebrews makes to the tradition concerning the obedience of Jesus consists of a creative understanding of the memory of Jesus's faithfulness. According to Hebrews, Jesus's faithfulness entailed a process of learning that, when brought to completion at his death, makes possible the eternal salvation of all who follow him, now empowered by the Son's perfection (5:8–10). But what specifically allows for this possibility? In other words, why did Jesus's own human response of faithfulness inaugurate a new way of encountering God (4:16)?

A potential clue to answering this question appears in the exordium, which depicts God commending the exalted and enthroned Son: "You loved justice and hated wickedness; therefore God, your God, anointed you with the oil of gladness above your companions" (1:9). Like other New Testament writings, Hebrews affirms the sinlessness of Jesus.[2] Twice Hebrews emphasizes this theme, first in 4:15, and then in 7:26. By linking this accent on the sinless character of Christ to the concept of education (5:8), Hebrews develops the traditional theme of Jesus's faithfulness into a strikingly new and original theological claim. The sinlessness of Jesus is envisioned as a trait that emerged in time and history because of the educative testing that the Son endured during his human career.[3] In other words, Hebrews conceives of the testing of Jesus as involving a learning experience (5:8), which enabled Jesus, the representative human being,

2. The idea is especially prominent in the writings of Paul: "For our sake he made him to be sin who did not know sin" (2 Cor 5:21).

3. See Heb 4:15; 12:2–3. David Peterson, *Hebrews and Perfection: An Examination of the Concept of Perfection in the Epistle to the Hebrews*, Society for New Testament Studies Monograph Series 47 (Cambridge: Cambridge University Press, 1982), 67.

to live out a fully human life in complete faithfulness to the will of God:

> For this reason, when he came into the world, he said:
>
> "Sacrifice and offering you did not desire,
> but a body you prepared for me;
> holocausts and sin offerings you took no delight in.
> Then I said, 'As it is written of me in the scroll,
> Behold, I come to do your will, O God.'"
> (10:5–7)

In declaring that the Son "came into the world" (10:5), Hebrews envisions not simply the final days of Jesus, but the entire life lived by the new great high priest. This was a life in which the Son embodied in a perfect or complete way the righteousness (1:9) belonging to God's kingdom in the form of concrete, selfless service to others (2:16). In living out this commitment to the fullest, Jesus also modeled for the first time an embodied human existence without sin. In turn, this wholehearted commitment of Jesus to embodying a life of righteousness, even to the point of death, was heard by God (5:7) who, in response to that commitment, established Jesus as the final exalted high priest:

> In the same way, it was not Christ who glorified himself in becoming high priest, but rather the one who said to him:
>
> "You are my son;
> this day I have begotten you";
>
> just as he says in another place:

> "You are a priest forever
> according to the order of Melchizedek." (5:5–6)

As a consequence of God's exaltation of Jesus—attesting to the divine vindication of the righteous life Jesus led—a new pathway is opened for the faithful to stand in God's presence (metaphorically conceived of as God's throne, 4:16). On the one hand, Hebrews thinks of this pathway as one made possible for others to travel because Jesus is now alive in a new way (10:19–20). On the other hand, what contributed to this pathway becoming a source of eternal salvation (5:9) in the first place was Jesus's perfect response of faithfulness, even to the point of death, which he demonstrated before God:

> Therefore, brothers and sisters, since through the blood of Jesus we have confidence of entrance into the sanctuary by the new and living way he opened for us through the veil, that is, his flesh, and since we have "a great priest over the house of God," let us approach with a sincere heart and in absolute trust, with our hearts sprinkled clean from an evil conscience and our bodies washed in pure water. (10:19–22)

This highly pastoral assurance of "a new and living way" of approach before the throne of God (4:16) first made possible by Jesus, the exalted great high priest, provides Hebrews' audience with a metaphorical "anchor of the soul, sure and firm which reaches into the interior behind the veil, where Jesus has entered on our behalf as forerunner, becoming high priest forever according to the order of Melchizedek" (6:19–20).

THE WITNESS OF SCRIPTURE TO A UNIQUE HIGH PRIEST (HEB 5:1-6)

Already we have seen something of the letter's rich and creative use of themes and terminology from the Jewish Scriptures to advance the author's priestly Christology. One scriptural resource that plays an especially outsized role in the Christology of Hebrews would have to be Psalm 110. We have already noted that, since the first Christ followers were ethnically and religiously Jews, they turned quite naturally to the Jewish Scriptures to help them come to terms with the suffering, death, and resurrection of Jesus. Among the many texts consulted for this task by the first Christ followers, the Book of Psalms supplied an especially powerful resource for articulating the array of experiences engendered by the Christ event. Particularly meaningful were the psalms of lament, which picture righteous Jews suffering persecution at the hands of the unrighteous precisely because of their whole-hearted commitment to God. Passages from such important texts as Psalm 22 and Psalm 69 provided ready-made templates for affirming the innocence of Jesus, thus empowering early Christ followers to cope with the trauma of the crucifixion.

But the tragic death of Jesus was not the only event pressing for explanation. Early Christ followers also sought texts to help them make sense of the new life given to Jesus in his resurrection. Psalm 110 was perhaps the most frequently used by early Christ followers when interpreting the event of God's vindication of Jesus. Hebrews follows the tradition that interprets the opening verse of Psalm 110 as foreshadowing the royal exaltation of Jesus as God's promised messiah. While agreeing with this assessment, Hebrews reads beyond verse 1 and also applies verse 4 of the psalm to Jesus: "The LORD has sworn and will not waver: 'You are a priest forever in the manner of Melchizedek'" (Ps 110:4). In its original context, Psalm 110:4 celebrates the Israelite king's reception of a priestly status that complemented his royal one. Hebrews invests this verse with new meaning, first by interpreting the nameless priest as Jesus, and second by interpreting the "forever" part of the priestly epithet as pointing to the resurrection of God's Son.

Already the exordium of Hebrews hints at the importance Psalm 110 will play in the Christology of the letter (see 1:3, 15). Since this psalm is so integral to the priestly Christology of Hebrews, it merits some preliminary comments. In its original historical context, Psalm 110 celebrated the divine investiture of royal power given to the Israelite king to act on behalf of the God of Israel (110:1). This power encompassed not only military dominance, but also a priestly prerogative (110:4). As we have explained, one of the functions of the exordium is to empower the audience to enter imaginatively into the sacred space of the heavenly sphere where God is portrayed as receiving the exalted Jesus into heaven (1:5–12). We have also noted how this scene functions to underline the Son's superiority to the angels. Now we see Hebrews quote for the first time a specific passage from Psalm 110, a passage that will serve as the basis for the author's further presentation of Jesus as an eternal high priest throughout the rest of the letter (6:20; 7:17; 8:1; 10:12; 10:22): "just as he says in another place: 'You are a priest forever according to the order of Melchizedek'" (5:6).

Although numerous writings from the New Testament viewed Psalm 110 as foretelling Christ's exaltation (e.g., Mark 12:35–37; Matt 22:43–44; Acts 2:29–35; 1 Cor 15:25; 1 Pet 3:22), interest in this royal psalm among early Christ followers was limited principally to the psalm's opening line: "The LORD says to my Lord: 'Sit at my right hand, while I make your enemies your enemies your footstool'" (110:1). Hebrews appears to have been the first to have read further along in the Psalm and to have discovered still another promise that had been fulfilled by Jesus. Guided by the assumption that the authentic meaning of Scripture is fulfilled in the coming of Jesus, Hebrews sees the promise of Jesus's vindication wedded to a divine oath testifying to the appearance of a priestly figure of an entirely different order, the mysterious order of Melchizedek (5:6, 10; 6:20; 7:11, 17, 21). More will be said about the significance of Melchizedek in the next chapter. For now, it is important to recognize that one of the reasons why Hebrews is drawn to Psalm 110:4 is because it helps the author address the difficulty that surrounds the troublesome lack of a priestly lineage for Jesus. That is, Psalm 110:4 supplies Hebrews with the scriptural attestation of God's promise that another priest would arise, one whose priesthood would not be derived from Levitical descent:

> If, then, perfection came through the Levitical priesthood, on the basis of which the people received the law, what need would there still have been for another priest to arise according to the order of Melchizedek, and not reckoned according to the order of Aaron? (7:11)

We might say, therefore, that the superiority of Christ's priestly status rests not only on the sinlessness revealed through the human faithfulness of God's Son, but also on the divine oath that promised a high priestly status as a consequence of the exaltation of God's Son.

Hebrews continues to pursue the development of its high priestly Christology by drawing an explicit comparison between the high priesthood of Jesus and that of human high priests:

> Every high priest is taken from among [humans] and made their representative before God, to offer gifts and sacrifices for sins. He is able to deal patiently with the ignorant and erring, for he himself is beset by weakness and so, for this reason, must make sin offerings for himself as well as for the people. No one takes this honor upon himself but only when called by God, just as Aaron was. In the same way, it was not Christ who glorified himself in becoming a high priest, but rather the one who said to him:
>
> "You are my son;
> this day I have begotten you";
>
> just as he says in another place:
>
> "You are a priest forever
> according to the order of Melchizedek." (5:1–6)

This passage opens with the noncontroversial claim that every high priest is appointed from the ranks of the community and given the responsibility to engage in sacrificial activity before God (5:1; see also 8:3). Hebrews proceeds to note, however, that the choice of the human high priest is nevertheless subordinated to a prior divine appointment. Not just any member of the covenant community can serve as a priest: "No one takes this honor upon himself but only when called by God, just as Aaron was" (5:4). According to Scripture, the God of Israel had selected Aaron and his sons to be the Lord's anointed priests (see Exod 28:1); thereafter, the priesthood was to be a perpetual status based on hereditary lineage lasting for all generations to come (Exod 40:12–15). As we have just seen, Hebrews affirms that the high priestly status of Jesus also rests on a divine appointment; but, in this instance, the appointment was not inherited but came directly from God and was confirmed with a divine oath: "In the same way, it was not Christ who glorified himself in becoming high priest, but rather the one who said to him: 'You are my son; this day I have begotten you'" (5:5). Hebrews will make a similar point later in chapter 7: "And to the degree that this happened not without the taking of an oath—for others became priests without an oath, but he with an oath, through the one who said to him: 'The Lord has sworn, and he will not repent: "You are a priest forever"'" (7:20–21).

Hebrews contrasts the priesthood of Jesus versus that of the Levitical high priests. The Levitical priests had an indirect and corporate calling, by virtue of their human lineage, whereas Jesus received a direct and unique calling by God. Hebrews also contrasts the emotive stance of Jesus versus that of the Levitical high priest. Earlier Hebrews described Jesus, the great high priest, as motivated by empathy or compassion toward humanity. Now Hebrews attaches a particular emotive stance to the Levitical high priest: this priest "is able to deal patiently" with fellow sinful human beings, since even he "himself is beset by weakness" (5:2). For this reason, Hebrews points out, the Levitical high priest "must make sin offerings for himself as well as for the people" (5:3).

It appears that Hebrews wishes to forge a connection between the Levitical high priest's emotive response of patience and the reality of sin. But what is this connection? The key appears to involve weakness, a term that appeared for the first time in Hebrews 4:15. According to Hebrews, the high priest can show patience with fellow human beings because, like them, he shares the experience of being bound by sin (5:2). The Son, while fully human in every way, is unlike other humans to the degree that he is sinless. For all their exalted status, human high priests are still acquainted with sin, something which Hebrews conceives of as a weakness (5:2). The qualitative difference between the Levitical priesthood and the priesthood of Jesus revolves on this point. Although tempted to sin, Jesus remained faithful. In contrast, human high priests are susceptible to the weakness of sin that "besets" them (5:2), which makes it necessary for them to offer sacrifices not only for others but also for themselves. The argumentative logic here is driven less by an explicit criticism of human high priests than the positive uniqueness of God's Son. Jesus is unique in that he is both an exalted high priest and a sinless high priest, one who in his status as the risen Lord displays compassion, not just patience, for sinful humanity with whom he has identified as the representative human being.

CHAPTER 4

Jesus, the Eternal High Priest

In the previous two chapters, we have focused primarily on exploring the human dimension of the priestly Christology of Hebrews. Whether by highlighting the Son's solidarity with humanity, or by identifying the perfect response of faithfulness to God that Jesus displays during his public ministry, Hebrews emphasizes the fundamental role of Jesus's humanity for properly understanding the kind of a high priest Jesus is. We have also made the point, however, that much of the real achievement of Hebrews lies in the considerable balance within its Christology between the human and exalted aspects of Jesus's identity as a high priest. Beginning in chapter 7, and continuing through the middle of chapter 10, Hebrews expends increasingly more effort reflecting on the role that Jesus's exaltation plays in his qualification as high priest. Yet, even in this section of the letter, the author continues to give attention to the human-centered sacrificial activity of Jesus. In this final chapter, we will trace the contours of this blended christological image and explore the ways in which it contributes to the theological beauty and pastoral power of Hebrews.

A PRIEST ACCORDING TO THE ORDER OF MELCHIZEDEK (HEB 7:1–28)

This final stage in the development of the priestly Christology of Hebrews begins with the author's commentary on the mysterious figure of Melchizedek. On two previous occasions Hebrews has referred to Melchizedek (5:10; 6:20), but only now is the audience given more detail about his role and identity:

> This "Melchizedek, king of Salem and priest of God Most High," "met Abraham as he returned from his defeat of the kings" and "blessed him." And Abraham apportioned to him a "tenth of everything." His name first means righteous king, and he was also "king of Salem," that is, king of peace. Without father, mother, ancestry, without beginning of days or end of life, thus made to resemble the Son of God, he remains a priest forever. (7:1–4)

The mysterious figure of Melchizedek is mentioned in only two places in the Jewish Scriptures (Gen 14:18–20 and Ps 110:4), and in both instances tantalizingly little information is given about him. The passage from Genesis is the more detailed of the two occurrences. There Melchizedek is introduced as the mysterious priest-king of Salem who meets the patriarch Abraham upon the latter's return from a campaign of military conquest. What follows next is an act of reciprocal giving between the two figures. The reader learns that Melchizedek blessed Abraham and bestowed upon him the gifts of bread and wine (Gen 14:18–19), while Abraham, for his part, gave a tithe to Melchizedek (Gen 14:20). Melchizedek makes an even briefer appearance in Psalm 110. We have already discussed the importance of this psalm for early Christ followers who saw in its opening verse the promise of the future event of the exaltation of Jesus: "The LORD says to my Lord: 'Sit at my right hand, while I make your enemies your footstool'" (Ps 110:1). As we have seen, Hebrews reinterprets this psalm by focusing on the untapped theological significance of a later verse (Ps 110:4).

THE FIGURE OF ABRAHAM IN THE NEW TESTAMENT

While Abraham is mentioned in several New Testament texts (e.g., Matt 1:1; John 9:53–56), the New Testament author most associated with Abraham is the Apostle Paul. In two of his letters (Galatians and Romans), Paul points to Abraham as exemplar of the response of faith that makes one rightly aligned with God ("righteous"). In Galatians, Abraham is presented as an exemplar for Gentiles, while in Romans Paul highlights Abraham's significance for both Jews and Gentiles.

> Realize then that it is those who have faith who are children of Abraham. Scripture, which saw in advance that God would justify the Gentiles by faith, foretold the good news to Abraham, saying, "Through you shall all the nations be blessed." Consequently, those who have faith are blessed along with Abraham who had faith. (Gal 3:7–9)

> And he received the sign of circumcision as a seal on the righteousness received through faith while he was uncircumcised. Thus, he was to be the father of all the uncircumcised who believe, so that to them [also] righteousness might be credited, as well as the father of the circumcised who not only are circumcised but also

> follow the path of faith that our father Abraham walked while still uncircumcised. (Rom 4:11–12)

Hebrews is not the only Second Temple Jewish text to show interest in the figure of Melchizedek. Some writings reflected on the symbolic significance of Melchizedek's name (7:1–2); others examined the figure of Melchizedek from a more cosmic perspective.[1] Whether or not the author of Hebrews was familiar with such texts, clearly the figure of Melchizedek was of great thematic importance. Two primary reasons account for this. First, the Genesis account connects Melchizedek, the priest-king of Salem, to the biblical figure of Abraham, someone who functions in Hebrews (as in other New Testament writings) as a symbolic figure of origins. That is, Hebrews affirms the scriptural portrayal of Abraham as the great biblical patriarch to whom God made a promise to bless his descendants and to make of them his people (6:13–15; cf. Gen 12:2–3; 22:16). Hebrews finds particular significance in the scriptural notice that Abraham, the heir to the promise, not only received a blessing from Melchizedek, but also gave a tithe to the mysterious priest king of Salem:

> See how great he is to whom the patriarch "Abraham [indeed] gave a tenth" of his spoils. The descendants of Levi who receive the office of priesthood have a commandment according to the law to exact tithes from the people, that is, from their brothers, although they also have come from the loins of

1. Eric F. Mason, "Cosmology, Messianism, and Melchizedek: Apocalyptic Jewish Traditions in Hebrews," in *Reading the Epistle to the Hebrews: A Resource for Students*, ed. Eric F. Mason and K.B. McCruden, Resources for Biblical Study 66 (Atlanta: Society of Biblical Literature, 2011), 53–76.

> Abraham. But he who was not of their ancestry received tithes from Abraham and blessed him who had received the promises. Unquestionably, a lesser person is blessed by a greater. (7:4–7)

Recalling the earlier comparison between Jesus and Moses, Hebrews finds in the encounter between Abraham and Melchizedek nothing less than a divine intimation that confirms the superior status of Melchizedek to Abraham. Moreover, since Abraham can be reckoned as a forebear of the future line of Levitical priests (7:5), Hebrews declares that Melchizedek in some fashion received tithes from the hereditary priesthood yet to come:

> But he who was not of their ancestry received tithes from Abraham and blessed him who had received the promises. Unquestionably, a lesser person is blessed by a greater. In the one case, mortal men receive tithes; in the other, a man of whom it is testified that he lives on. One might even say that Levi himself, who receives tithes, was tithed through Abraham, for he was still in his father's loins when Melchizedek met him. (7:6–10)

This line of reasoning makes it possible for Hebrews not only to claim a higher status for Melchizedek with respect to Abraham, but a higher status with respect to the Levitical priesthood as well: "If, then, perfection came through the levitical priesthood, on the basis of which the people received the law, what need would there still have been for another priest to arise according to the order of Melchizedek, and not reckoned according to the order of Aaron?" (7:11). In this way, Hebrews quite creatively addresses the knotty problem involving Jesus's lack of priestly lineage. According to

Hebrews, it was always the divine intention to inaugurate a completely unique order of priesthood that would one day replace the established Levitical order (7:11–12). According to Hebrews, Jesus is the high priest of this completely different—and superior—order.

The second reason why Hebrews is so intrigued by the figure of Melchizedek concerns the aura of mystery surrounding the origin of the enigmatic priest king of Salem. Building upon the etymology of Melchizedek's name, Hebrews notes,

> His name first means righteous king, and he was also "king of Salem," that is, king of peace. Without father, mother, or ancestry, without beginnings of days or end of life, thus made to resemble the Son of God, he remains a priest forever. (7:2–3)

Noticing that Melchizedek appears suddenly in Scripture without any mention of his origin or hereditary background, Hebrews perceives in Melchizedek an icon or representation of timelessness:

> Now he of whom these things are said belonged to a different tribe, of which no member ever officiated at the altar. It is clear that our Lord arose from Judah, and regarding that tribe Moses said nothing about priests. It is even more obvious if another priest is raised up after the likeness of Melchizedek, who has become so, not by a law expressed in a commandment concerning physical descent but by the power of a life that cannot be destroyed. For it is testified:

> "You are a priest forever
> according to the order of Melchizedek."
> (7:13–17)

The unique priesthood God had intended all along was to be eternal, a priesthood that endured forever (Ps 110:4). Hebrews understands this new eternal priesthood to be prefigured in the Psalm's language of the "likeness" of Melchizedek (7:15). It is crucial, however, to appreciate the precise direction in which Hebrews applies the "likeness" of Melchizedek to Christ (7:13). Inspired by the faith commitment shared with other early Christ followers, Hebrews affirms the gospel message that Jesus has been raised from the dead and now lives in a new way in the presence of God (13:20). In other words, the everlasting life into which Jesus entered upon his exaltation is the lens through which the idea of the "likeness" of Melchizedek is viewed, not the other way round. Melchizedek is like Christ to the degree that a shadow might be said to bear the muted outline of the one who casts it. Once again, we see Hebrews employing the tool of comparison—in this case, a comparison between the nature of the high priesthood of Jesus and that of ordinary priests. Only now the comparison has less to do with the sinlessness of Jesus than with the eternal status of Jesus's high priesthood:

> Those priests were many because they were prevented by death from remaining in office, but he, because he remains forever, has a priesthood that does not pass away. Therefore, he is always able to save those who approach God through him, since he lives forever to make intercession for them. (7:23–25)

THE FIGURE OF MELCHIZEDEK IN SECOND TEMPLE JUDAISM

Like the author of Hebrews, the Jewish philosopher Philo of Alexandria shows an interest in the etymological significance of the name Melchizedek. Unlike Hebrews, however, Philo is most interested in the symbolism associated with authentic kingship than with timelessness: "Moreover, God made Melchizedek, the king of peace, that is, of Salem, for that is the interpretation of this name, 'his own high priest,' without having previously mentioned any particular action of his, but merely because he had made him a king, and a lover of peace, and especially worthy of priesthood. For he is called a just king, and a king is the opposite of a tyrant, because the one is the interpreter of the law, and the other of lawlessness" (Philo, *Allegorical Interpretation*, 3.25).

The prominence Hebrews gives to the motif of the eternal status of the high priest Jesus adds another layer to the theme of the weakness of the Levitical high priesthood first introduced in chapter 5 (5:2–3). Whereas there the weakness envisioned by Hebrews pertained to the reality of sin that encompassed the human high priest, now the weakness that is envisioned centers on the susceptibility to death (7:28). As a consequence of his obedience to God, Jesus was exalted to the right hand of God (8:1). The eternal life that Jesus shares with God entails an existence no longer limited by death. Since Jesus now lives forever, it follows that his high priestly sacrifice is eternal as well:

> It was fitting that we should have such a high priest: holy, innocent, undefiled, separated from sinners, higher than the heavens. He has no need, as did the high priests, to offer sacrifice day after

> day, first for his own sins and then those for the people; he did that once for all when he offered himself. For the law appoints men subject to weakness to be high priests, but the word of the oath, which was taken after the law, appoints a son who has been made perfect forever. (7:26–28)

THE TRUE SANCTUARY AND THE OFFERING OF JESUS (HEB 8—10)

In the previous chapter, we explained that Hebrews strives to celebrate with its audience the communal confession that Jesus is the great high priest who has "passed through the heavens" (4:14). This theme of the exaltation of Jesus, announced anew in Hebrews 7, now serves as the consistent backdrop throughout chapters 8 through 10. These chapters complement the theme of Jesus's exaltation and eternal status by focusing repeatedly on the appearance of the risen Jesus in the heavenly sanctuary. There, in the presence of God, the risen Jesus offers a one-time sacrifice for sin (9:11–14, 24–28; 10:11–18). In a sense, Hebrews returns in these chapters to the very beginning of the sermon (1:1–14) when the audience was first encouraged to witness the moment when Christ enters the heavenly sphere to appear before the presence of God:

> The main point of what has been said is this: we have a such a high priest, who has taken his seat at the right hand of the throne of the majesty in heaven, a minister of the sanctuary and of the true tabernacle that the Lord not [any human being], set up. Now every high priest is appointed to offer gifts and sacrifices; thus the necessity for

> this one also to have something to offer. If then he were on earth, he would not even be a priest, since there are those who offer gifts according to the law. They worship in a copy and shadow of the heavenly sanctuary, as Moses was warned when he was about to erect the tabernacle. For he says, "See that you make everything according to the pattern shown you on the mountain." (8:1–5)

Once more we see Hebrews developing its Christology against the narrative background of the Jewish Scriptures, this time with the account of the wilderness sanctuary. According to the Book of Exodus, God instructs Moses to have the people create a portable tabernacle in the wilderness (Exod 25:1–9) complete with an altar for the purpose of sacrifice (27:18). Exodus consistently notes that the tabernacle itself and the various elements contained within it—such as the ark of the covenant (25:22), the table for the showbread (25:23–30), and the menorah (25:31–40)—all are to be crafted in accordance with the plan God revealed to Moses (25:9, 40; 26:30; 27:8). Hebrews lavishes attention on many of the items mentioned in the Exodus account:

> For a tabernacle was constructed, the outer one, in which were the lampstand, the table, and the bread of offering; this is called the Holy Place. Behind the second veil was the tabernacle called the Holy of Holies, in which were the gold altar of incense and the ark of the covenant entirely covered with gold. In it were the gold jar containing the manna, the staff of Aaron that had sprouted, and the tablets of the covenant. Above it were the cherubim of glory overshadowing the place of expiation. (9:2–5)

Into this sanctuary and beyond, to the inner space called the "Holy of Holies," the high priest alone enters on the annual Day of Atonement. Similar to how the author deals with the figure of Melchizedek, Hebrews envisions the wilderness sanctuary of long ago through the lens of an ideal, heavenly sanctuary that exists outside of space and time: "For Christ did not enter into a sanctuary made by hands, a copy of the true one, but heaven itself, that he might now appear before God on our behalf" (9:24). Thus, like the exalted Jesus, this heavenly tabernacle is eternal, not limited to the created realm (9:11). And just as the high priest is said to enter the earthly wilderness sanctuary to make atonement for sins (9:6–7), so Christ also enters the ideal sanctuary that exists in heaven:

> But when Christ came as high priest of the good things that have come to be, passing through the greater and more perfect tabernacle not made by hands, that is, not belonging to this creation, he entered once for all into the sanctuary, not with the blood of goats and calves but with his own blood, thus obtaining eternal redemption....How much more will the blood of Christ, who through the eternal spirit offered himself unblemished to God, cleanse our consciences from dead works to worship the living God. (9:11–14)

The language employed by Hebrews, in this as well as in other passages in this section of the letter (see 8:1–2; 9:11, 23; 10:19–20), shows the strong influence of a specific way of thinking about reality pervasive in antiquity. Derived ultimately from the Greek philosopher Plato, this way of thinking conceived of what is truly real as eternal and invisible, as opposed to what is visible and changeable. The latter, while "real" to some degree, was a mere shadow of the former.

Given the influence of this conceptual model on Hebrews, it is striking that the emphasis on the exaltation of Jesus above is then balanced by a very different emphasis, namely the humanity of Jesus:

> Therefore, it was necessary for the copies of the heavenly things to be purified by these rites, but the heavenly things themselves by better sacrifices than these. For Christ did not enter into a sanctuary made by hands, a copy of the true one, but heaven itself, that he might appear before God on our behalf. Not that he might offer himself repeatedly, as the high priest enters each year into the sanctuary with blood that is not his own; if that were so, he would have had to suffer repeatedly from the foundation of the world. But now once for all he has appeared at the end of the ages to take away sin by his sacrifice. (9:23–26)

In this passage as well as in 9:13–14 and 10:19, a thematic contrast arises between, on one hand, the blood offered by Jesus, and the sacrificial blood of animals offered by the high priest, on the other. The contrast hinges on Hebrews' conviction that the sacrifice offered by Jesus was a deeply personal one and therefore unique:

> But when Christ came as high priest of the good things that have come to be, passing through the greater and more perfect tabernacle not made by hands, that, is not belonging to this creation, he entered once for all into the sanctuary, not with the

> blood of goats and calves but with his own blood, thus obtaining eternal redemption. (9:11–12)

As noted earlier in this study, in the Christology of Hebrews the sacrificial actor is comingled with the one sacrificed. Through this image the author of Hebrews emphasizes the human faithfulness that Jesus displayed before God. Through his life of deeply personal and faithful obedience to God (9:14), Jesus made possible a new way of encountering God in the new age, one that entails the transformation of the heart through the cleansing of conscience (9:14; 10:1–3, 19–22).

While Hebrews presents the exalted Jesus and his sacrifice against the eternal backdrop of a heavenly and eternal sanctuary, Hebrews also celebrates with its audience the shared conviction that the exalted Son is precisely the one who showed perfect faithfulness to God in a deeply personal way, involving his deepest self: "how much more will the blood of Christ, who through the eternal spirit offered himself unblemished to God, cleanse our consciences from dead works to worship the living God" (9:14). The true achievement of the priestly Christology of Hebrews is disclosed in how it blends what seem to be two very different dimensions of the Christ event into a dynamic whole without resolving the theological tension between the two. The Letter to the Hebrews articulates nothing less than a portrait of Jesus the great high priest that holds in harmonious tension the two poles that together make up the mystery of the Christ event. Perhaps more eloquently than any other writing in the New Testament, Hebrews shows that, without the exaltation of Jesus, the Son could not be the source of eternal salvation (5:9). The life of faithful and personal obedience that Jesus displayed before God is the very foundation of the Son's exaltation.

TRANSFORMATION AND RENEWAL OF THE HEART AND MIND

In addition to the encouragement that Hebrews' audience may have drawn from hearing the title of high priest applied to Jesus, there are other examples of pastoral care found in Hebrews. Here I am thinking of the evident task of identity formation that Hebrews pursues in the hopes of shaping the values and habits of mind of its audience. Such shaping of identity is especially clear in those sections of the letter where Hebrews repeatedly emphasizes how Christ's sacrificial activity in the heavenly sanctuary has resulted in the renewal and cleansing of individual hearts and minds:

> In this way the holy Spirit shows that the way into the sanctuary had not yet been revealed while the outer tabernacle had its place. This is a symbol of the present time, in which gifts and sacrifices are offered that cannot perfect the worshiper in conscience. (9:8–9)
>
> ...How much more will the blood of Christ, who through the eternal spirit offered himself unblemished to God, cleanse our consciences from dead works to worship the living God. (9:14)
>
> Since the law has only a shadow of the good things to come, and not the very image of them, it can never make perfect those who come to worship by the same sacrifices that they offer continually each

> year. Otherwise, would not the sacrifices have ceased to be offered, since the worshippers, once cleansed, would no longer have any consciousness of sins? (10:1–2)

> And since we have "a great high priest over the house of God," let us approach with a sincere heart and in absolute trust, with our hearts sprinkled clean from an evil conscience and our bodies washed in pure water. (10:21–22)

The pastoral power of such passages becomes clearer when viewed in light of the priestly Christology of Hebrews explored in this study. As we have seen, Hebrews finds supreme importance in Jesus's own response of faithfulness, even going so far as to depict Jesus as having offered himself to God through "the eternal spirit" (9:14). This stress on the perfect commitment of Jesus to walk the obedient path of fulfilling God's will (5:7; 10:8–10) empowers a similar quality of interiority and cleansing for the renewal of the hearts and minds of the faithful. Inasmuch as the high priesthood of Christ touches on a harmony between the exalted and the human, so the efficacy of the risen Jesus's offering in the heavenly sanctuary reaches deeply into the inner lives of the faithful. What happens in heaven happens within the hearts and minds of believers. Anchored to this reality of renewal, and confident in their fellowship with Christ (3:1, 14), the faithful are given the strength to continue to look to Jesus as the "leader and perfector of faith" (12:2).

Hebrews grounds the reality of such a capacity for transformation and renewal in the end-time prophecy found in the prophet Jeremiah:

> Behold, the days are coming, says the Lord,
> when I will conclude a new covenant with the
> house of Israel and the house of Judah....
> But this is the covenant I will establish with the
> house of Israel
> after those days, says the Lord:
> I will put my laws in their minds,
> and I will write them upon their hearts.
> I will be their God
> and they shall be my people. (8:8–10)

In a quotation taken almost word-for-word from Jeremiah (Jer 31:31–33), Hebrews declares that the prophet's ancient promise of a new relationship of covenantal intimacy between God and the people of Israel is now at hand because of the sacrifice of Christ:

> Now he has obtained so much more excellent a ministry as he is mediator of a better covenant enacted on better promises. For if that first covenant had been faultless, no place would have been sought for a second one. (8:6–7)

Jesus's sacrifice in the heavenly sanctuary, which also demonstrated the transparency of his spirit to God's will (10:5–9), makes possible a new covenant and a renewed relationship with God: "For this reason he is a mediator of a new covenant: since a death has taken place for deliverance from transgressions under the first covenant, those who are called may receive the promised eternal inheritance" (9:15). Spoken to an audience that still found themselves living this side of the age to come in a situation of distress (see 10:32–36; 12:7–13), the sermonic Letter to the Hebrews undoubtedly inspired hope in its audience as much as it expanded their thinking about the identity of Jesus. Hopeful that, in their worship and common life with one another, they could meet God even now within the inner depths of their lives, the author and first hearers of Hebrews celebrated a foretaste of the salvation they looked to inherit soon (2:10, 14; 9:28). This was a salvation made possible by the new and living way inaugurated by Jesus, the great high priest, who passed through the heavens (4:14), but nonetheless is always near (7:25).

Conclusion

The Contemporary Relevance of Hebrews' Priestly Christology

In this study we have explored the high priestly Christology of Hebrews, especially where the human dimension of Christ's high priesthood is placed prominently on display. We have seen that the distinctiveness of Hebrews lies in the way it invites its audience to reflect on received theological and christological traditions (like exaltation, incarnation, and atonement) in new and creative ways. The Letter to the Hebrews gives unique expression to an exalted understanding of Christ in which the risen Jesus is portrayed as an eternal high priest who offers in a heavenly sanctuary a deeply personal sacrifice that yields abiding atonement. What makes this high priestly portrait of Jesus so unique, however, is the care the author takes in crafting a sermon that honors fully the human and divine aspects of Christ. While Hebrews does not articulate in any formal sense the mystery of how Christ can be said to be both fully divine and fully human, it does insist that the human career of Jesus must always be regarded as intrinsically connected to the exalted status of Christ. Although the Son is described in Hebrews as exalted above the angels and as the speech that articulates God, the same Son also displays profound solidarity with human beings. Hebrews takes seriously that the Son's acquaintance with the human condition was a thoroughly embodied one.

I would like to end this study on the priestly Christology of Hebrews by reflecting briefly on the world in front of the text: that is, the question concerning the potential relevance of Hebrews for today. Throughout this study, we have explored some of the specific ways in which Hebrews celebrates the depths of the Son's solidarity with humanity. As we have seen, Hebrews makes a point of emphasizing such solidarity even in those places where a more exalted portrait of Christ appears. Although Hebrews begins by depicting God's Son as the definitive revelation of God and Creator of the cosmos, much of Hebrews' preoccupation in this, as well as later chapters, is to show how very near to humanity the risen Christ remains. Hebrews tells us of a divine Son who, as the representative of humanity (2:5–9), participates to the fullest possible degree in the flesh and blood existence of human beings. Indeed, the latter are described as siblings of Jesus (2:5–14), as well as the sole focus of divine care (2:16). We are also reminded that the divine mission of the Son is to ultimately guide humanity to glory. But even now, in the present, God's Son liberates the faithful from fear of death (2:15) and captivity to sin (2:17). The Son's solidarity with humanity extends even to providing a reassuring model to those facing testing of their own with the Son's own experience with a testing that led to death.

The theme of Christ's intimate solidarity with humanity bears a striking similarity to the teachings of Jesus that we encounter in the canonical Gospels concerning the true nature of divine power. Whether by employing parables that focus on the importance of reconciliation (Luke 19:1–10), or by imparting teachings that exalt the pattern of serving others instead of being served (Mark 10:42–46), the Jesus we meet with in the Gospels envisions a way of living and being in the world defined by radical identification with others. To the degree that the priestly portrait of Christ in Hebrews complements the portrayal of Jesus elsewhere in the New Testament, it can serve as a paradigm for our own interpersonal relationships. Hebrews affirms that Christ partook of a fully embodied human existence as the singular pathway for fulfilling the divine intention to bring all humankind to glory. Such an affirmation should challenge us to recognize how so often parochial and highly selective are our own attempts to identify with those whom we regard as our brothers and sisters. The high priestly Son of God, pictured in Hebrews as greater than the angels and as enthroned beside God as a heavenly high priest, is also the Son who fully identifies with humanity, liberating everyone for a communal journey to final end-time glory with God.

Another facet of Hebrews' Christology that has potential relevance for today is the insistence that the sacrificial activity of Jesus within the heavenly sanctuary has a bearing on the inner lives of the faithful. The priestly Christology of Hebrews reminds us that the death and resurrection of Jesus is, at heart, an empowering event. This becomes especially evident in those passages in the letter where our author links the sacrificial work of Christ to the cleansing of the conscience of the faithful (9:9, 14; 10:19–22). One way to conceive of this cleansing is to connect it with sinful activity on our part in the past, now forgiven through Christ, the great high priest. But Hebrews' theme of the transformation of the conscience of the faithful points to something else: Christ's sacrifice provides not only for the forgiveness of sin (10:11–12) but also the consecration of the believer (10:10, 14). Perhaps this is at least part of what Hebrews is getting at when it portrays Christ as the high priest who even now and forever intercedes on our behalf as the great high priest (7:23, 25). What such consecration implies is that believers, both then and now, are liberated to live a different kind of life, empowered by the life of faithfulness before both God and neighbor that was first enacted fully by Jesus.

Select Bibliography

Attridge, Harold W. *The Epistle to the Hebrews: A Commentary on the Epistle to the Hebrews*. Hermeneia. Philadelphia: Fortress, 1989.

Carvalho, Corrine L. *Primer on Biblical Methods*. Winona: Anselm Academic, 2009.

DeSilva, David A. *The Letter to the Hebrews in Social-Scientific Perspective*. Cascade Companions. Eugene, OR: Cascade, 2012.

Eusebius. *Eusebius' Ecclesiastical History*. Translated by C. F. Cruse. Repr., Peabody, MA: Hendrickson, 1998.

Gelardini, Gabriella, ed. *Hebrews: Contemporary Methods – New Insights*. Biblical Interpretation Series 75. Leiden: Brill, 2005. Repr., Atlanta: Society of Biblical Literature, 2008.

Gordon, Richard. "The Veil of Power: Emperors, Sacrificers, and Benefactors." In *Pagan Priests: Religion and Power in the Ancient World*, edited by Mary Beard and John North, 201–31. Ithaca, NY: Cornell University, 1990.

Greer, Rowan A. "The Jesus of Hebrews and the Christ of Chalcedon." In *Reading the Epistle to the Hebrews: A Resource for Students*, edited by Eric F. Mason and and Kevin B. McCruden, 231–49. Resources for Biblical Study 66. Atlanta: Society of Biblical Literature, 2011.

Irenaeus. *The Ante-Nicene Fathers*. Edited by Alexander Roberts and James Donaldson. 1885–1887. 10 vols. Repr., Peabody, MA: Hendrickson 1994.

Johnson, Luke Timothy. *Hebrews: A Commentary*. New Testament Library. Louisville, KY: Westminster John Knox, 2006.

Koester, Craig R. *Hebrews: A New Translation with Introduction and Commentary*. Anchor Bible 36. New York: Doubleday, 2001.

Lindars, Barnabas. *The Theology of the Letter to the Hebrews*. New Testament Theology. Cambridge: Cambridge University Press, 1991.

Maier, Harry O. "For Here We Have No Lasting City" (Heb 13:4a): Flavian Iconography, Roman Imperial Sacrificial Iconography, and the Letter to the Hebrews." In *Hebrews in Contexts*, edited by Gabriella Gelardini and Harold W. Attridge, 133–54. Ancient Judaism and Early Christianity 91. Leiden: Brill, 2016.

Mason, Eric F., and Kevin B. McCruden, eds. *Reading the Epistle to the Hebrews: A Resource for Students*. Resources for Biblical Study 66. Atlanta: Society of Biblical Literature, 2011.

McCruden, Kevin B. *A Body You Have Prepared for Me: The Spirituality of the Letter to the Hebrews*. Collegeville, MN: Liturgical, 2013.

———. *Solidarity Perfected: Beneficent Christology in the Epistle to the Hebrews*. BZNW 159. Berlin: De Gruyter, 2008.

McMahon, Christopher. *Reading the Gospels: Biblical Interpretation in the Catholic Tradition*. Winona, MN: Anselm Academic, 2012.

Mitchell, Alan C. *Hebrews*. Sacra Pagina 13. Collegeville, MN: Liturgical Press, 2007.

Moffitt, David M. *Atonement and Logic of the Resurrection in the Epistle to the Hebrews*. Supplements to Novum Testamentum 141. Leiden: Brill, 2011.

Peterson, David. *Hebrews and Perfection: An Examination of the Concept of Perfection in the Epistle to the Hebrews*.

SNTSMS 47. Cambridge: Cambridge University Press, 1982.

Philo. *The Works of Philo*. Translated by C. D. Yonge. Peabody, MA: Hendrickson, 1993.

Reed, Annette Yoshiko. "Hellenistic Judaism beyond Judaism and Hellenism." In *Above, Below, Before, and After: Studies on Judaism and Christianity in Dialogue with Martha Himmelfarb*, edited by Ra'anan Boustan, David Frankfurter, and Annette Yoshiko Reed, 15–42. Tübingen: Mohr Siebeck, 2023.

Sanders, E. P. *Paul and Palestinian Judaism: A Comparison of Patterns of Religion*. Philadelphia: Fortress, 1977.

Scholer, John M. *Proleptic Priests: Priesthood in the Epistle to the Hebrews*. Journal for the Study of the New Testament Supplement Series 49. Sheffield: JSOT Press, 1991.

Thompson, James W. *Strangers on the Earth: Philosophy and Rhetoric in Hebrews*. Eugene, OR: Cascade, 2020.

Vanhoye, Albert. *The Letter to the Hebrews: A New Commentary*. Translated by Leo Arnold, SJ. New York: Paulist Press, 2015.

———. *Old Testament Priests and the New Priest According to the New Testament*. Trans. J. Bernard Orchard. Petersham: St. Bede's Publications, 1986.